To

Fr

C000153468

Thank you for your help?

FEBRUARY
1942

Dedication

To Judith and Craig.
Here's hoping for many happy returns.

FEBRUARY 1942

Britain's Darkest Days

ADRIAN STEWART

Pen & Sword
MILITARY

First published in Great Britain in 2015 by
PEN & SWORD MILITARY
an imprint of
Pen & Sword Books Ltd
47 Church Street
Barnsley
South Yorkshire S70 2AS

ISBN 978 1 47382 115 6

A CIP catalogue record for this book is
available from the British Library.

Typeset in Ehrhardt by Chic Graphics

Printed and bound in England
by CPI Group (UK) Ltd, Croydon, CR0 4YY

Pen & Sword Books Ltd incorporates the imprints of
Pen & Sword Archaeology, Atlas, Aviation, Battleground, Discovery,
Family History, History, Maritime, Military, Naval, Politics, Railways,
Select, Social History, Transport, True Crime, Claymore Press,
Frontline Books, Leo Cooper, Praetorian Press, Remember When,
Seaforth Publishing and Wharncliffe..

For a complete list of Pen & Sword titles please contact
PEN & SWORD BOOKS LIMITED
47 Church Street, Barnsley, South Yorkshire, S70 2AS, England
E-mail: enquiries@pen-and-sword.co.uk
Website: www.pen-and-sword.co.uk

Contents

Maps

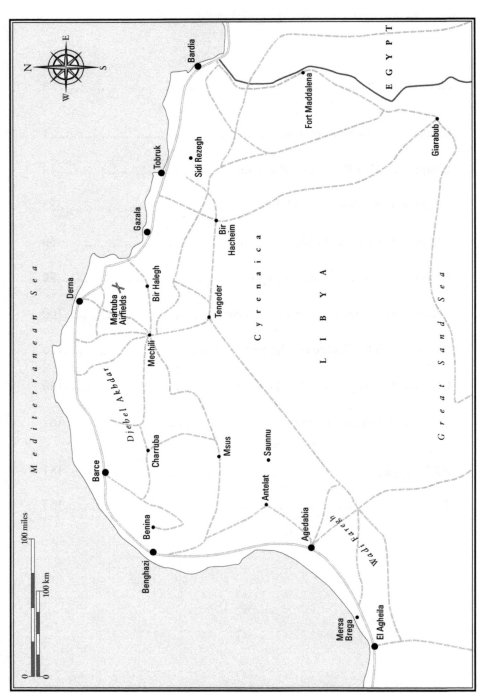

The return of Rommel.

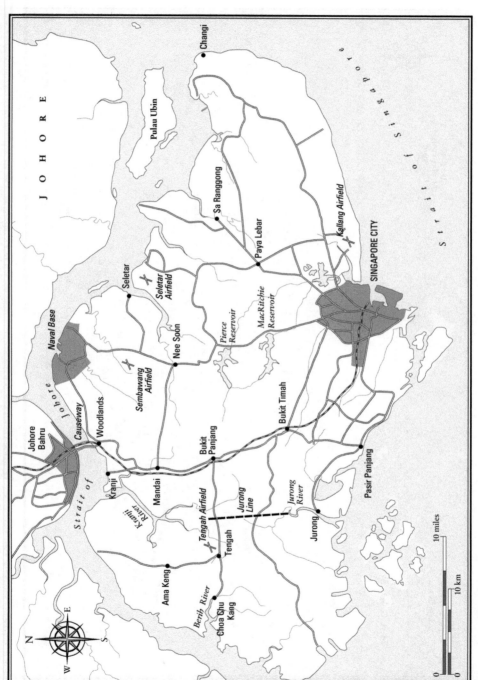

Singapore Island.

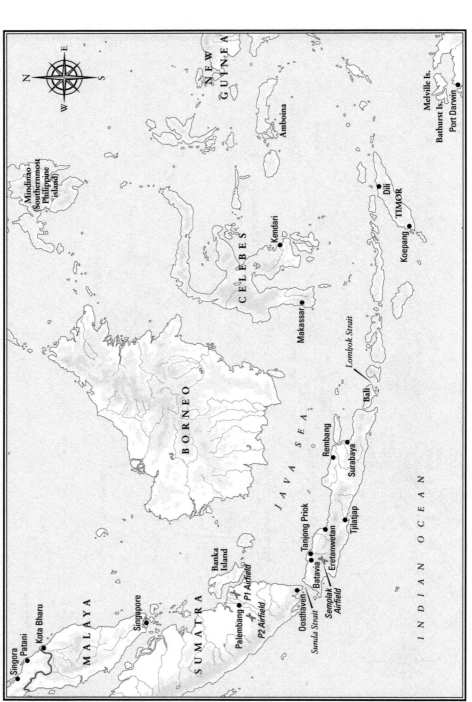

The East Indies and the approaches to north-western Australia.

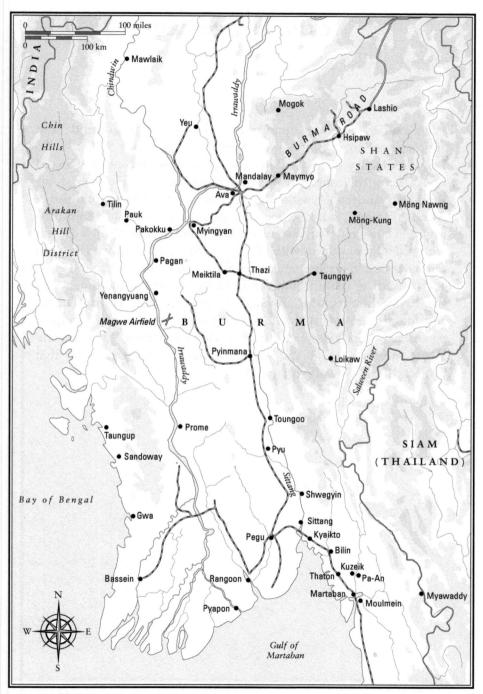

The Japanese invasion of Burma.

Acknowledgements

I am glad to have the opportunity to express my gratitude and appreciation to a number of kind and necessary helpers. To Brigadier Henry Wilson and his team at my publishers, Pen & Sword Books Limited, especially my indispensable liaison officer, Matt Jones. To Andrew Hewson and his team at my Agents, Johnson & Alcock Limited, who advice was particularly valuable this time round. To my indefatigable editor and proof reader, Pamela Covey, who had a lot to put up with. To Sylvia Menzies-Earl, who as usual did me proud in her preparation of the manuscript. To Philip Fisher and the staff of the Birmingham Institute & Library, and the staff of the Taylor Library who provided the photographs. To the authors and publishers of the works mentioned in the Bibliography, particularly Sir Winston Churchill, whose history of 'The Second World War' has to be the starting point for all research on that subject. Thank you all very much.

Chapter 1

The Background

President Franklin Roosevelt must have had difficulty believing his eyes. He had received a letter from Winston Churchill that showed the prime minister, for so long the inspirer and symbol of Britain's defiance in the face of adversity, to be deeply pessimistic. It began with a most uncharacteristic lament: 'When I reflect how I have longed and prayed for the entry of the United States into the war, I find it difficult to realise how gravely our British affairs have deteriorated by what has happened since December 7 [1941].' It mentioned British setbacks in North Africa and the Far East, the increasing danger to Malta, and the problems caused by a shortage of shipping. It warned that 'other misfortunes will come thick and fast upon us.'

Admittedly the prime minister did state that 'All can be retrieved in 1943 and 1944' – though an earlier (and later) Churchill would have said 'will be retrieved' – but even then he felt compelled to add that in the meantime there would be 'very hard forfeits to pay'. That Roosevelt was concerned by the tone of Churchill's message is shown by the fact that shortly afterwards, he sent his friend and ally an exhortation to keep up his optimism and his driving force, tactfully veiled under a declaration that he knew this would be the case. It was not an admonition that anyone had ever needed to make to Churchill previously.

Yet Churchill had every reason for being despondent. He had written to Roosevelt on 5 March 1942 and the previous February had been a dismal catalogue of Allied, and particularly British, disasters in every theatre of war. The two months before February had been bad enough but they had at least brought some important achievements to set against the calamities.

Thus the most vital factor in December 1941 for the people of Britain and for Churchill in particular was, undoubtedly and rightly, the knowledge that, following the Japanese attack on Pearl Harbor on the 7th, the vast industrial power of the United States would be fully committed on their side. 'We had won after all!' declared the exultant prime minister. 'We are all in the same boat now,' Roosevelt remarked more soberly. Such was the joy and relief that little time was spent in reflecting that if Britain had gained an invaluable ally, she had also acquired a new and formidable foe.

Undoubtedly the main reason for this was that neither the armed services nor the general public had any idea of just how formidable their new foe was. Air Chief Marshal Sir Robert Brooke-Popham, Commander-in-Chief, Far East, had visited Hong Kong in 1940, at which date the Japanese were in occupation of the adjoining Chinese mainland. He scornfully described the Japanese troops stationed on the frontier as 'sub-human specimens dressed in dirty grey uniform' and announced that Hong Kong could hold out for at least six months if attacked. General Sir Archibald Wavell, who was Commander-in-Chief, India at the time of Pearl Harbor, considered that Japanese soldiers were very little superior to the Italians whom he had defeated in North Africa and especially liable to be confused by 'bold counter-offensive'.

Such views could and should have been corrected by good Intelligence but this was completely lacking. The Far Eastern Combined Intelligence Bureau at Singapore, under Admiralty control but receiving and supplying information from and to all three armed services, was contemptuous of the Japanese army's equipment, training and leadership, and considered that its soldiers 'had been grossly flattered as to their fighting efficiency by the feeble opposition available in China'. For good measure it added that they did not like night-fighting and, with a rather horrible irony considering how often they would outflank and outmanoeuvre British and Commonwealth troops in Malaya and Burma, that they 'preferred to advance along main roads'.

Opinions about the Japanese navy were less optimistic but again poor Intelligence made accurate assessment impossible. Neither the British nor the Americans were, for instance, aware of the lethal liquid oxygen-powered 'Long Lance' torpedoes carried by Japanese cruisers and destroyers that could deliver a warhead twice the size of that of their Allied equivalents at a far greater speed for a far longer distance. Nor had they any idea of the efficiency of Japan's carrier-based air force. As late as April 1942, Vice Admiral Sir James Somerville, an officer with considerable experience of naval air warfare, could not believe that the Mitsubishi Zero fighters, Aichi 'Val' dive-bombers and Nakajima 'Kate' torpedo-planes[1] were the standard equipment of Japanese 'flat-tops'.

Of all the Japanese forces, though, the Imperial Army Air Force was the most underrated. James Leasor in *Singapore: The Battle that Changed the World* remarks that 'the general opinion in Malaya was that the Japanese aircraft were made of rice-paper and bamboo shoots.' No doubt this was merely a witticism that would shortly prove most unamusing but even official publications solemnly related that the Japanese were no more than imitators and their aircraft were mere copies of Western ones and some five years out of date, much as would later be said of Japanese cars and motor-cycles, though not by those who owned them.

How ingrained was this attitude appeared most clearly at a meeting of the British chiefs of staff, no less, on 25 April 1941. The Vice-Chief of the Naval Staff, Rear Admiral Sir Tom Phillips, was certainly not an admirer of Japanese aircraft, considering them of much the same standard as those of Italy's Regia Aeronautica and 'markedly inferior' to those of the Luftwaffe. Nor was he concerned about the effect of air attacks on warships at sea, for he was confident these could always be repelled. Nonetheless, he believed that proper fighter protection should be provided, particularly for the great naval base at Singapore. He therefore recommended that Hawker Hurricanes, already appearing in large numbers in the Mediterranean theatre, should be sent to Malaya as well.

The suggestion was curtly rejected: Air Chief Marshal Sir Wilfred Freeman, Vice-Chief of the Air Staff, declared that it was unnecessary to provide Malaya with Hurricanes as the American Brewster Buffalo fighters already stationed there would be 'more than a match' for Japanese aircraft. His attitude was echoed by the airmen in the Far East. Brooke–Popham publicly stated that Buffaloes were 'quite good enough for Malaya'. Air Vice–Marshal Conway Pulford, commanding the RAF in Malaya, claimed that Japanese aircraft were inferior to those of the Italians, let alone those of the Germans. In reality, it was the slow, unmanoeuvrable Buffaloes that were inferior to most Italian aircraft. They were unworthy opposition even for Japanese bombers, while a Buffalo pilot who attempted to dog-fight with Japanese fighters would be very lucky if he survived the encounter.

Once again the Far Eastern Combined Intelligence Bureau did not correct but instead supported these comforting assurances. Indeed it went further, for it derided not only the Japanese machines but also Japanese airmen. The latter, it appears, all suffered from defective eyesight that made it impossible for them to make low-flying attacks, bomb accurately or conduct any operations after dark.

In consequence, the news of early Japanese successes caused as much bewilderment as shock, and there were many such successes in December 1941. For the British, the worst of the bad news were the Japanese invasions of Hong Kong and Malaya and the sinking of the new battleship *Prince of Wales* – too new, for her hectic early career had given her no opportunity of reaching full fighting efficiency – and the aging battle-cruiser *Repulse* by Japanese shore-based naval aircraft.

The loss of Hong Kong, which formally surrendered on Christmas Day – though some isolated units continued the fight until the early hours of the 26th – can have caused little surprise. In fact its garrison, cut off from all chance of help and faced with a capable, well-trained enemy who enjoyed a significant superiority in manpower, a strong superiority in artillery and a total superiority in the air, may well be thought to have resisted longer than anyone had a right to expect. Certainly Churchill was unlikely to have been astonished. Probably his main regret was that just three weeks before Japan went to war with Britain, two inexperienced and ill-equipped Canadian battalions had arrived at Hong Kong where they were duly sacrificed. They had been sent by the chiefs of staff against

Churchill's own wishes on the urgings of a Canadian officer, Major General A. Edward Grasett, who had previously commanded in Hong Kong and shared Brooke-Popham's low opinion of the Japanese army.

By contrast, Churchill was shocked by the sinking of *Prince of Wales* and *Repulse* on 10 December. That, though, was partly because he was very conservative in naval matters and had not, it seems, appreciated the major change that had been taking place in the previous year and of which Pearl Harbor afforded the final confirmation, namely that aircraft carriers, not battleships, would be the main naval weapon of the future.

It is further noticeable that Churchill's confidence in ultimate victory now that the United States was in the war was in no way affected by the sinking of *Prince of Wales* and *Repulse*. He did, however, rightly appreciate that Britain might have to suffer further as a result of their loss, because this gave Japan command of the waters around the Malay Peninsula and hence the ability to transport troops there without interference.

The initial Japanese landings were made at Kota Bharu in the extreme north-east of Malaya and at Singora and Patani in the Kra Isthmus just north of this in Thailand (or Siam as it was then also known). At the same time, Japanese land forces from Indo-China, which was already occupied by them, poured over the border into central Thailand, whereupon that country collapsed forthwith and soon after made a treaty of alliance with Japan. Japanese airmen were as prompt as their soldiers and Army Air Force units were swiftly transferred to Singora and Patani, ready to support the assault on Malaya.

It had been hoped that the defenders of Malaya would also be supported by aircraft based on the twelve airfields that had been constructed in the north of the country as well as on fourteen more in other parts. Unfortunately, Air Vice-Marshal Pulford controlled only thirteen squadrons spread throughout Malaya and equipped with just 158 aircraft, mostly varying from elderly to obsolete: there were, for instance, four squadrons of the useless Buffalo fighters and two of Vildebeest biplane bombers, the top speed of which was optimistically assessed at 100 mph. Moreover, the enemy warplanes at Singora and Patani quickly launched attacks on the northern British aerodromes, effectively crippling Pulford's bomber force. As early as the evening of 9 December, he decided he had no choice but to withdraw his remaining machines. The Japanese had won a command of the air that they were never to lose.

This advantage was greatly aided by an unforgivable failure on the part of the British to make the abandoned airfields untenable. They were soon to be overrun by the Japanese advance and were found to be fit for operations either at once or after a few days and to contain large caches of stores that should have been destroyed. Soon Japanese aircraft based on captured British aerodromes and flying on captured British fuel were dropping captured British bombs on British and Commonwealth soldiers.

There were many other difficulties facing Malaya's ground troops. They considerably outnumbered their opponents but this advantage was largely neutralized because they were widely scattered over the whole peninsula, often in dangerously exposed locations. Even greater problems were their lack of training and their lack of quality.

Lieutenant General Arthur Percival, the head of Malaya's land forces, controlled ten brigades in total. Of these, two weak Malayan brigades were stationed on Singapore Island and the 22nd and 27th Australian brigades of 8th Australian Division remained in the Sultanate of Johore in the extreme south of the peninsula. The other six were all Indian brigades: three of these were in the north, two in central Malaya and one in the south.

Despite their name, Indian brigades were not manned wholly by Indians, for it was usual practice that one battalion in every brigade should be British. Nonetheless, the men of the remaining two battalions did come entirely from India – apart from those of Gurkhas from the independent kingdom of Nepal – as did their Viceroy's commissioned officers (VCOs)[2] and NCOs, while a growing number of their officers were also Indians; there were 500 of these in 1939 and 8,300 by 1945. In all, during the Second World War well over 2 million Indians fought for Britain, every one of them a volunteer.

Sadly, however, the Indian battalions in Malaya had less than a

year's service behind them and to make matters worse had been
'milked', as it was called – 'bled' would be a more accurate
description – by being deprived of their officers, VCOs and NCOs,
who had been sent to the new units being raised in India. They were
quite untrained in jungle warfare and quite unused to modern
warfare of any kind. The Japanese had medium and light tanks in
Malaya. Both types were six or more years old, cramped, with
inadequate protective armour and equipped with one 57mm gun and
two machine guns or one 37mm gun and two machine guns
respectively. Yet their effect on raw recruits who had never so much
as seen a tank before can be imagined.

As if all of that was not enough, the British and Commonwealth
soldiers were given two different tasks that were mutually
incompatible. They were supposed to delay the enemy for as long as
possible, thereby giving time for reinforcements to reach Singapore
so that it could hold firm and then be used as a base for a counter-
offensive. On the other hand, they had to preserve their own strength
so that they could form part of Singapore's garrison in due course.

In practice, the result was that when the more mobile Japanese
outflanked their British and Commonwealth opponents, the latter
would avoid the risk of being cut off by a hasty retirement, often in
disorder and leaving behind vital stores that fell into the hands of
their enemies, who jestingly called them 'Churchill's allowance'. Nor
were there any strong positions to which the defenders could fall
back or on which they could make a stand, since the authorities had
forbidden any to be constructed in the belief that this would be bad
for morale. It may be wondered, however, whether this could
possibly have been as damaging as a continuous series of retreats,
each one of which further sapped the will of the soldiers.

By the end of December, the British had fallen back some 150
miles from their original forward positions and the New Year saw
only a continuation of the same depressing pattern. The 8th
Australian Division under the arrogant, aggressive Major General
Henry Gordon Bennett was now sent into action. A new Indian
brigade and a new British brigade – 18th Division's 53rd Brigade –
reached Malaya and were hastily added to the number of the
defenders. Yet while the Japanese advance was checked occasionally,

it was never halted. Nor could attacks on Japanese motor transport by a handful of Hurricanes that had arrived on 13 January and been made ready for action a week later do more than delay the invaders' progress, though Japanese sources speak admiringly of the 'serious challenge' posed by 'their intrepid pilots'. By 27 January, all British and Commonwealth ground troops were in full retreat towards Singapore Island.

This was, by now, a somewhat dubious refuge, though the fact was scarcely appreciated in Britain where it was confidently maintained that Singapore was 'an impregnable fortress', 'the bastion of Empire', 'the Gibraltar of the East'; the same, indeed, was still being repeated, if in increasingly desperate tones, in Singapore itself. Churchill had, until recently, entertained a similar belief. His confidence had begun to waver as he learned the details of the island's lack of prepared fortifications but he still thought that reinforcements must be sent to it and that it could and should hold out for a considerable time. The setbacks in January, therefore, had alarmed him but not yet dented his own steadfast optimism.

What really sustained the morale of the prime minister and of the country as a whole, however, was that, as mentioned earlier, the news in December 1941 and January 1942 was not all bad. On 19 January, in a telegram to John Curtin, Prime Minister of Australia, Churchill pointed out that while matters in the Far East were going badly, the Allies could all be thankful not only that the United States had entered the war but for victories gained in Russia and against the German-Italian forces commanded by General Erwin Rommel in North Africa.

In Russia, a final German attempt to reach Moscow petered out on 2 December 1941 in ever-worsening weather and on the same day, the Russians struck forward from Rostov at the extreme south of the battle lines to begin an advance of 40 miles. On the 6th, they advanced both north and south of Moscow as well. They were clothed, equipped and trained for fighting in the steadily increasing cold, whereas the Germans enjoyed none of these advantages and in early December, some of their units suffered casualties from frostbite five times higher than those inflicted by their enemies. It was a potentially catastrophic situation.

A disastrous defeat greater than that of Napoleon in 1812 was, in fact, averted only by Adolf Hitler. Though his obstinacy would cost Germany dearly on later occasions, it now saved his army from annihilation. He refused to consider retiring one step more than he was absolutely compelled to and dismissed or accepted the resignation of any senior commander who urged withdrawal. All the same, during the remainder of the year and throughout January 1942, the Russians steadily drove back the invaders all along their huge front line, in some sectors for more than 150 miles. Many German infantry divisions were reduced to almost one-third of their original numbers and losses of armour, aircraft and equipment generally were also immense. These could never be fully replaced and Hitler could only bring his army up to strength by reinforcing it with Italian, Hungarian and Rumanian troops of inferior quality.

Compared with these Russian achievements, the Allied successes in North Africa were of less importance. Since, however, they were gained by British and Commonwealth troops they proved very cheering to Britain and her Dominions as the self-governing parts of the British Empire were then called. They were particularly gratifying for Churchill because he had deliberately risked calamities in the Far East for the sake of ensuring them.

On 6 May 1941, the then Chief of the Imperial General Staff, General Sir John Dill, had reminded the prime minister that: 'It has been an accepted principle in our strategy that in the last resort the security of Singapore comes before that of Egypt. Yet the defences of Singapore are still considerably below standard.' Dill was therefore much concerned by Churchill's expressed intentions of building up his forces in Egypt regardless of the needs of the Far East. His anxiety was shared by military and naval experts in the United States and in July, Roosevelt had also sent warnings to Churchill of the risks he was running by concentrating all his attention on North Africa. Churchill, though, had ignored every argument, for he was convinced that he would be able to drive the enemy out of North Africa and gain a victory that would 'rank with Blenheim and with Waterloo'.

Accordingly, much to Churchill's satisfaction, massive reinforcements originally designated for the Far East were instead dispatched to Egypt, enabling General Sir Claude Auchinleck, Commander-in-Chief, Middle East, to build up his strength in readiness for Churchill's longed-for offensive. This began on 18 November 1941 and was rather dramatically code-named Operation CRUSADER.

By that date, the war in the Western Desert, a harsh wasteland that covered most of Egypt and the then Italian colony of Libya, had already lasted almost two-and-a-half years, during which time the fighting had swung continually backwards and forwards. First had come an Italian invasion of Egypt. Next a British offensive had driven the enemy out of Egypt and gone on to overrun the whole of Cyrenaica, Libya's eastern province. Finally a counter-offensive by German troops, sent by Hitler to Italy's aid and led by General Erwin Rommel, had brought the front line back to the Egyptian/Cyrenaican border. It had thus recovered all the Italian losses save for the isolated port of Tobruk, the garrison of which, supplied from the sea, posed a constant threat to Rommel's own supply lines.

This was not Rommel's only disadvantage at the start of CRUSADER. The opposing forces were roughly equal in numbers but most of the Axis infantrymen were Italians whose inadequate equipment and desperate shortage of motor vehicles meant they could only be used in a static role. By contrast, all the infantry divisions in the British Eighth Army, as it had formally become at midnight on 26 September, were properly mechanized. In armour, the British advantage was even greater. Eighth Army had 710 gun-armed tanks, plus 500 more in reserve. Rommel had no reserves, his 146 Italian tanks were obsolete and of little value, and of his 250 German tanks, some 70 were in effect armed only with machine guns since the 20mm gun that they carried was useless in a tank-on-tank encounter and a further 35 could fire only high-explosive shells, devastating against infantry but unsuitable for use against hostile armour. Rommel's adverse position was, however, partly mitigated by his excellent anti-tank guns with a penetrative power superior to that of their British equivalents and indeed that of the German armour.

Eighth Army's supporting air arm, officially known as the Western Desert Air Force, though in practice the word 'Western' was rarely used, was also superior to its opponents. It could muster some 500 serviceable machines and call up considerable reserves from the Nile Delta in time of need. Rommel, by contrast, could rely on the assistance of only some 300 serviceable warplanes, of which not much more than a third were German. In addition, the Axis ground and air forces alike were dangerously short of supplies, especially petrol.

Despite all these problems, to which were added the offensive attaining complete surprise and the heaviest rainstorm of the year flooding the Axis airfields but not those of the Desert Air Force, Rommel fought back viciously. CRUSADER became a series of complicated, confused encounters, with little apparent progress and a good deal of blundering on both sides. Fortunately both Churchill and Auchinleck were sustained by the knowledge that their enemies were limited in strength, short of supplies and without hope of reinforcements, all of which were revealed by intercepted signals, the famous 'Ultra' Intelligence.

On 7 December, the day of the attack on Pearl Harbor, these disadvantages finally induced Rommel to acknowledge defeat. All his troops, except those in his strongpoints on the frontier who had been cut off from the main Axis army, now fell back. Eighth Army had won its first victory and if it was scarcely one to rank alongside Blenheim or Waterloo, it was still very welcome. Further good news to offset that from the Far East came in from North Africa during the remainder of the month, as the British continued their advance, ultimately to El Agheila on the border between Cyrenaica and Libya's western province of Tripolitania. In the circumstances, it was understandable that few cared to reflect that Rommel's army had not been destroyed, even temporarily, as a fighting force and had retired in good order to a very strong position. Nor did anyone remark that Auchinleck's pursuit had not been particularly impressive.[3]

There was more good news in the New Year. As mentioned, Rommel's retreat had abandoned his troops in the frontier positions. The reduction of these was entrusted to Eighth Army's reserve formation, 2nd South African Division, aided by 1st (British) Army Tank Brigade. On 2 January, the garrison in Bardia surrendered. On the 12th, the Axis defences in the area of Solium were taken. On the

17th, the last outpost, Halfaya, fell. In all, 13,800 Axis soldiers were taken prisoner and at Bardia 1,177 Allied soldiers who had been captured during the course of CRUSADER were liberated.

It appeared, moreover, that these successes would not be the last. Auchinleck had begun to plan an Eighth Army advance to Libya's capital, Tripoli, code-named Operation ACROBAT. He was confident that this would present few difficulties, assuring Churchill that the Axis troops who had survived CRUSADER were 'divisions in name only', were 'much disorganized, short of senior officers, short of material' and with their morale 'beginning to feel the strain', were 'hard pressed, more than we dared think perhaps'.

But then everything began to go horribly wrong.

Notes

1. The Allies avoided the difficulties of the complicated Japanese system of aircraft classification, made worse by poor pronunciation, by giving each type an arbitrary code-name: ladies' names for the bombers; men's names for the fighters. Mitsubishi's famous naval fighter, however, proved the exception. The year when it had gone into production, 1940, was the Japanese year 2600, counting from the legendary foundation of the country by its first Emperor, Jimmu Tenno, in 660 BC. In Japan it was referred to by the last two numbers of this year and so became Type 00 or 'Zero Sen'. The Allied airmen almost always called it the Zero as well, or in the case of RAF pilots the Navy Nought, not the Zeke which was its official code name.
2. Viceroy's Commissioned Officers were roughly akin to the warrant officers of the British army but enjoyed the additional privilege of being saluted by their men, though not by the British troops.
3. Eighth Army in fact took thirty days to cover the 470 miles by the coast road to El Agheila. After its victory at El Alamein in November 1942, Eighth Army took only nineteen days to advance 840 miles by the coast road to El Agheila, and has been roundly condemned for dilatory progress.

Chapter 2

The Return of Rommel

Although Rommel's brilliant response to CRUSADER began in January 1942, its success was not certain until the following month and it was then that it gained its most important strategic prize. It seems fair, therefore, to consider it the first of those calamities that made 'Black February' Britain's worst month of the Second World War.

It was preceded by a difference of attitude between Churchill and his Commander-in-Chief, Middle East that would in itself cause problems for the future. It is surprising to find Churchill, of all people, adopting a cautious stance, but having in effect bartered the security of the Far East for triumph in North Africa, he was understandably troubled by any suggestion that Eighth Army's success might prove only fleeting and he had been warned by Ultra that supplies and reinforcements were at last reaching Rommel.

Auchinleck also knew all about Rommel's reinforcements from Ultra but he appears to have been unconcerned. He sent Churchill those cheerful assurances that were recounted earlier, and on 19 January told his subordinates that his intention was 'to continue the offensive in Libya and the objective remains Tripoli.' Two days later, an offensive was duly launched, but not by Auchinleck.

That Rommel's counter-offensive followed so swiftly on Auchinleck's assurances shook Churchill's faith in his C-in-C, Middle East. This in turn resulted in a flood of warnings, complaints and questions from the prime minister. They were always well-intentioned but were often unfair or unreasonable and they increasingly distressed and worried Auchinleck. 'In the end,' says

General Sir David Fraser in his history of the British army in the Second World War *And We Shall Shock Them*, 'all confidence between them expired.' 'The fault,' adds Fraser, 'was not only Churchill's.' It was not a healthy situation and it was not the only unsatisfactory aspect of the British position in the Western Desert in early 1942.

General Sir Claude Auchinleck was a tall, well-built, distinguished man whose natural dignity and charm inspired affection as well as respect. In his previous role of Commander-in-Chief, India, he had become almost a father figure to his Indian soldiers, in whom he was genuinely interested, about whom he was very knowledgeable and for whose welfare he was immensely and conscientiously concerned. As a result, he ensured that, despite civil discontent, his men, coming from all parts of the subcontinent, were alike in their continuing loyalty to the King-Emperor.

Unfortunately, as Dill (a personal friend of Auchinleck) realized, that officer was not well qualified for the post that he now held and for which, it is only fair to emphasize, he had never expressed the slightest desire. He had had little experience of the conditions he would meet in the Western Desert and, as the Australian war correspondent Alan Moorehead points out in his book *The Desert War*, he 'believed that he could control the battle from Cairo.' Unhappily, the quick-moving, fast-changing actions in Egypt and Libya were 'not geared to remote control'.

To conduct the campaigns on his behalf, Auchinleck relied on loyal subordinates who would follow his advice and be there to take the responsibility if matters went badly. As Eighth Army Commander for CRUSADER, Auchinleck, ignoring the concerns of Churchill and the chiefs of staff, had appointed Lieutenant General Sir Alan Cunningham, who had proved very successful against the Italians in East Africa but lacked experience of armoured warfare or indeed of any warfare against Germans. For Auchinleck, however, this was of less importance than the fact that Cunningham was a friend who was most unlikely to disregard his wishes.

Auchinleck not only chose an inexperienced army commander, but presented him with the plan on which he was to fight his battle. As the British *Official History*[1] makes clear, this plan was prepared by

Auchinleck's staff; it was personally approved by him after he had examined it 'very thoroughly' and had 'weighed every conceivable course open to Rommel', and it was a thoroughly bad one.

In essence the idea was that Eighth Army would sweep round the southern flank of Rommel's frontier positions and then, while these were engaged by the bulk of the Allied infantry, Eighth Army's famous 7th Armoured Division would destroy the German panzers, after which the relief of Tobruk, the reconquest of Cyrenaica and the advance to Tripoli would all follow as a matter of course. Yet as Captain B.H. Liddell Hart points out in his *History of the Second World War*, 'an armoured force is not in itself suited to be an immediate objective. For it is a fluid force, not easily fixed as infantry formations can be.' An attempt to track down this elusive target was likely to result in the British armour becoming dispersed and vulnerable to counter-attack.

Nor did the plan give any indication as to how the British armour might achieve its aim. The only suggestion offered was that 7th Armoured Division should proceed to a point called Gabr Saleh, though this had no practical importance and was chosen simply because it was a convenient landmark on which to rally in an otherwise featureless area of desert. Here 7th Armoured would halt and wait to see what action its enemies would take; in other words, would surrender all initiative to Rommel.

As was perhaps inevitable, the battle became a series of thrusts and counter-thrusts and Cunningham, unused to the ebb and flow of fighting in the desert, became almost ill from worry, exhaustion and depression. By 23 November, his chief staff officer Brigadier Alexander 'Sandy' Galloway and Eighth Army's two corps commanders, Lieutenant Generals Godwin-Austen and Willoughby Norrie, were, says Field Marshal Lord Carver, then a member of Norrie's staff, in his *Dilemmas of the Desert War*, much 'concerned at both the physical and the mental state' of their leader. They therefore persuaded him to request that Auchinleck come to his headquarters and discuss the situation.

Happily, earlier on the same day, Auchinleck had received both from Churchill and from Ultra interceptions the encouraging news that Rommel's supply situation was becoming desperate. On arriving at Eighth Army's headquarters that evening, he therefore forbade the withdrawal that Cunningham was considering but Galloway, Godwin-Austen and Norrie were strongly opposing, and dismissed Cunningham on 26 November. Cunningham would later fill a number of important offices with distinction but would never receive another operational command.

Auchinleck had now to appoint a new Eighth Army commander and again his choice was surprising. It is usually stated that Auchinleck was a poor judge of men but this was not really the case. Many of his selections appear positively inspired; none more so than his appointment of the future Major General Sir Francis de Guingand first as his Director of Military Intelligence, later as the Brigadier General Staff of Eighth Army. De Guingand, for his part, was 'very fond' of his chief but he also came to appreciate the real motives that lay behind Auchinleck's choices: Auchinleck preferred subordinates who would meet his wishes without question over those, however talented, whom he thought too independently-minded. As de Guingand put it, Auchinleck had a 'desperate need' for 'loyal courtiers'.

Nobody could have been a more loyal courtier than the officer whom Auchinleck chose to replace Cunningham. This was his own Deputy Chief of the General Staff, Major General Neil Ritchie. He was a capable staff officer, determined, optimistic and energetic, but he had no personal experience of desert operations or of high command in battle. In addition, he was placed in a most invidious position because he was junior to both Godwin-Austen and Norrie. To his credit, Ritchie was most reluctant to accept his new post but Auchinleck was adamant. For him, Ritchie had one ideal qualification: as the *Official History* relates, if Ritchie knew his commander-in-chief's wishes, he 'was not the man to act otherwise than with energy and enthusiasm in giving effect to them.'

Ritchie's loyal attitude encouraged and strengthened Auchinleck's desire to control Eighth Army through a willing delegate and he spent a great deal of time at Eighth Army headquarters. On 1 December, for example, he began a visit to Ritchie that lasted for ten consecutive days, giving 'advice' that, as the *Official History* drily remarks, could hardly have had much distinction from 'orders'. Ritchie, who had urged Auchinleck to assume direct command of Eighth Army himself until a replacement could arrive from Britain, must have reflected ruefully that his suggestion had been largely carried out.

In practice, these problems did not matter too much so far as Operation CRUSADER was concerned, since provided this was not broken off, Eighth Army was certain to win, if only by attrition. It was after victory had been achieved that the peculiar command arrangements were to prove so harmful.

Having reached El Agheila, the British were faced with two major concerns. One was that in a desert, everything had to be supplied to the armies: not only petrol and ammunition, but food and water. To do this, they could use only two metalled roads: the Via Balbia in Libya, hugging the Mediterranean coast all the way from Tripoli to the Egyptian frontier, and the less well-constructed coastal highway in Egypt running from the frontier to Alexandria. Both were inadequate as well as extremely vulnerable to air attack.

In addition, the supplies had to be brought up over immense distances, which meant that the further an army advanced, the less easily it could be supplied and in consequence the weaker it became. Major General J.F.C. Fuller in *The Decisive Battles of the Western World* compares the lines of communication to 'a piece of elastic' that could only 'be stretched with comparative safety to between 300 and 400 miles from its base – Tripoli on the one hand and Alexandria on the other.' If it was stretched further, it might snap. Yet by the coast road Tripoli and Alexandria were almost 1,400 miles apart. This difficulty could only be endured but it meant that when Eighth Army pursued Rommel to El Agheila, it was compelled to keep Norrie's XXX Corps in the vicinity of Tobruk, leaving only Godwin-Austen's XIII Corps in the front line.

The other question facing Eighth Army was whether it would be better for XIII Corps to remain in close contact with the enemy at El Agheila, accepting the risk of being overextended, or to build up its strength at Agedabia some 40 miles north of El Agheila, or even further north at Benghazi or Msus. This latter action might mean giving up 150 miles of the ground Eighth Army had won, but most of this was only worthless desert.

In retrospect, it can be seen that yielding ground to gain security would have been the wiser choice and it was the one urged by a number of XIII Corps' officers. Auchinleck, however, took a different view. He was eager to launch ACROBAT as soon as possible and no doubt was conscious of Churchill's critical scrutiny. His decision – and once more the *Official History* confirms that it was his decision, not that of Ritchie who simply did what his chief wanted – resulted in the British formations being so widely dispersed that they presented Rommel with a tempting target that he had no desire to resist.

Stationed nearest to the enemy was Major General Frank Messervy's 1st Armoured Division, a recent arrival in the desert that was under strength and had been scattered over most of Cyrenaica. Furthest forward was one-half of the 200th Guards Brigade at Mersa Brega on the coast road and 1st Support Group some 20 miles inland around the Wadi el Faregh. Neither was particularly strong and both had been further weakened by being divided up into 'Jock Columns'.

Jock Columns were the creation of Brigadier John Charles 'Jock' Campbell, the inspirational leader of 7th Support Group, an infantry and artillery unit that formed part of 7th Armoured Division at the time of CRUSADER during which he had won a Victoria Cross.[2] They were small, highly mobile groups of motorized infantry and field guns that appealed to officers and men of active, individualistic temperaments. It is important, though, to note that Campbell intended that they should be used to raid, harass and confuse only; he declared frankly that they were incapable of capturing strong enemy positions or resisting strong enemy attacks.

Unfortunately, Auchinleck found them comfortingly familiar; he had known similar formations during his service in India. He therefore favoured their use on a wide scale and thus began a practice of splitting up British units that would become increasingly harmful. Since Jock Columns contained artillery, this arm, recognized even by the enemy as the most efficient in Eighth Army, was also unduly dispersed.

As Campbell would have been the first to warn, the 200th Guards Brigade columns and the 1st Support Group columns could not be expected to resist a counter-offensive by Rommel and the situation of the rest of 1st Armoured Division was not very inspiring either. The other half of the Guards Brigade was stationed at Agedabia and had no artillery since this had all been allocated to the Jock Columns. The 2nd Armoured Brigade, led by Brigadier Raymond Briggs, had had no experience of desert warfare and no training since leaving England for the Middle East; it was positioned between Antelat and Saunnu some 30 miles north-east of Agedabia. The 22nd Armoured Brigade, by contrast, had seen action in the later stages of CRUSADER and been badly mauled; it was back in Tobruk, re-equipping.

The other main formation in XIII Corps was Major General Francis Tuker's 4th Indian Division; really British-Indian Division for, as already described, one-third of its troops were British. Of its three brigades, the 7th, commanded, confusingly, by Brigadier Harold Briggs, was in Benghazi; the 5th was in Barce, north-east of Benghazi, where it was virtually immobile for lack of transport vehicles; and the 11th was in Tobruk. Godwin-Austen's XIII Corps HQ, incidentally, was in Msus, as were some supply units.

Against Eighth Army was ranged an Axis force commanded in theory by the Italian General Ettore Bastico but in practice by Rommel. For his counter-offensive the 'Desert Fox' could rely on little assistance from the Axis airmen, though this was at first balanced by the Desert Air Force being grounded; this time it was the British forward airfields that had been flooded by heavy rain. Rommel's five Italian infantry divisions played little part in his operations either. This would bring a curious benefit for Rommel, because when the Italian dictator, Benito Mussolini, sent his Chief of Armed Forces, General Ugo Cavallero, to North Africa to halt an offensive that he thought unwise, Rommel curtly retorted that German troops were bearing the brunt of the fighting, so the only person who could stop him was Hitler.

At dawn on 21 January 1942, to the amazement of the British higher command, Axis armour and motorized infantry fell upon the advanced units at Mersa Brega and Wadi el Faregh. A spearhead led by Lieutenant Colonel Marcks and coming mainly from the German 90th Light Division attacked along the coast road, backed by the rest of 90th Light under Major General Veith and with its right flank covered by Lieutenant General Gastone Gambara's XX Italian Corps containing the Ariete (Armoured) and Trieste (Motorized) divisions. The inland assault was entrusted to General Ludwig Crüwell's Afrika Korps, made up of 15th and 21st Panzer divisions.

Rather surprisingly in view of the weakness of the British units facing them, Rommel's men had little success on the 21st, finding the country they had to cross more difficult than expected. On the 22nd though, perhaps inspired by having formally received the ringing name of 'Panzerarmee Afrika', they broke through the Guards' defences on the Via Balbia. The 1st Support Group also fell back and the Axis infantry headed by the Marcks Group and closely followed by Crüwell's Afrika Korps struck northward, capturing Agedabia in the morning, Antelat in the afternoon and Saunnu in the evening.

These moves resulted in 1st Armoured Division's remaining infantry units and also its 2nd Armoured Brigade being cut off south-east of Antelat. Luckily, Rommel's attempts to destroy them on 23 January went badly wrong. The Marcks Group that had captured Saunnu headed south-east to attack the trapped forces in the flank, but the German armour that was supposed to take its place in Saunnu failed to do so. This gave 1st Armoured a chance to break out northward towards Msus. Aided by covering fire from the British artillery, Messervy's men duly escaped, though not without clashes with the panzers in which 2nd Armoured Brigade both suffered and inflicted losses.

This would seem a good moment at which to deal with the vexed question of tank superiority. Every British and Commonwealth soldier in the Middle East, from Auchinleck downwards, would maintain as an article of faith that British tanks were inferior to those of the Germans. It is not, however, a contention that bears detailed examination.[3]

Certainly Eighth Army's tanks had their faults. At the time of CRUSADER, the British had both heavy 'I' tanks, Matildas and Valentines,[4] and the lighter, faster cruiser tanks, Crusaders and American Stuarts, or 'Honeys', as their admiring crews called them. The 'I' tanks, particularly the now elderly Matildas, lacked speed, the Crusaders tended to be mechanically unreliable, and the Stuarts had only a short range. Yet because these disadvantages have been so often stressed, they have tended to mask the Allied tanks' superiority in the much more important fields of gun power and protective armour.

As mentioned earlier, the Germans at this period had three types of tank. Of these, the Mark II was useless in combat with British tanks, while the Mark IV was equipped with a short-barrelled low-velocity 75mm gun that fired not armour-piercing but high-explosive shells used mainly against infantry. Therefore the only real opponent of the British armour was the Panzer Mark III, carrying a short-barrelled, low-velocity 50mm gun that did fire armour-piercing shells. Careful tests conducted after the war, however, would confirm that this had less penetrative power than the 2-pounders used in all the British-built tanks or the equivalent 37mm in the Stuarts.

All German Mark IIIs and Mark IVs had been provided with 30mm armour over the entire hull and turret. This was considerably less than the armour on the Matildas with 78mm on the hull and 75mm on the turret or the Valentines that had 60mm on the hull and 65mm on the turret. As a result, both were virtually immune to the guns of enemy tanks except at very short range. The Crusaders had slightly less armour on the sides of their hulls (28mm), but their front hull plates (33mm) and turret armour (49mm) were thicker. The same was true of the Stuarts with 25mm armour on their sides, 44mm on their front hulls and 38mm on their turrets.

That their tanks' protective armour did not match that of their opponents was accepted by the Germans, who had therefore begun adding a further plate to the front of the hull. This doubled the width of armour and made the panzers superior in this respect to the Crusaders and Stuarts, though not to the heavy 'I' tanks. Their turrets, however, still remained vulnerable. Moreover, in the fury of battle, the Germans were unable to improve many tanks before the end of CRUSADER, although the ones that reached Rommel in January had already been so modified.

The reason for the frequent failures of the British armour was therefore not poor equipment but inappropriate tactics. It is usually said that the British dispersed their tanks too widely. This did happen but it is fair to add that it was not easy to achieve concentration in desert conditions and in any case, Rommel dispersed his armour, particularly during CRUSADER, far more widely than did Eighth Army. The real mistake made by Eighth Army was a failure to appreciate that, time and again, British tank casualties were caused not by the enemy armour but by the Germans' anti-tank guns. Their long-barrelled 50mms had a greater penetrative power than either the British 2-pounder anti-tank guns or the short-barrelled 50mms on the Germans' own Mark IIIs. The 88mm anti-aircraft guns, adapted to the role of tank-destroyers, were still more deadly and would earn a well-deserved and formidable reputation.

As a result of this misunderstanding, when Eighth Army's tank commanders tried to engage the enemy armour, they usually encountered enemy anti-tank guns instead; these were always used in combination with their own tanks, forming a defensive screen in front of them or pushing out boldly ahead of them if they were attacking. The Germans, by contrast, preferred to direct their armour against weaker targets such as supply echelons or unprotected infantry. This effective if unpleasant practice, combined with the exaggerated respect that Eighth Army paid to the panzers, meant that any unexpected moves made by these tended to cause considerable anxiety.

Thus 24 January 1942, a day that Rommel in practice wasted, doing nothing except hunt vainly for the troops south of Antelat who had already eluded him, was also a day when Eighth Army's senior commanders were loudly expressing their alarm. Godwin-Austen was particularly concerned that 1st Armoured Division, after its recent losses, would be unable to hold Msus and if it attempted to do so, might be severely mauled. On the other hand, if it retired too far, it would mean that 7th Indian Brigade at Benghazi might easily be cut off. The XIII Corps commander therefore asked Ritchie for permission to withdraw both his divisions to Mechili, north-east of Msus and due east of Benghazi, should this prove necessary.

Ritchie at first was less worried. He did give Godwin-Austen discretion to retire to Mechili if he was forced to do so, but gave his opinion that Rommel must have reached the limit of his advance and that XIII Corps should hold Benghazi and Msus if at all possible. In addition, though, he ordered XXX Corps up from the frontier to prepare a reserve defensive line running south from Gazala and protecting Tobruk; a prudent precaution but one that did not improve the confidence of his subordinates at this time of heightened tension.

Meanwhile, Churchill had also got to hear about what was taking place and sent to Auchinleck one of those signals that the C-in-C, Middle East must have come to dread, demanding to know what had happened and why retreat was necessary. This prompted Auchinleck to fly to Ritchie's HQ on 25 January. There he remained until 1 February and there he issued 'advice' that only made matters worse.

Also on the 25th, Rommel resumed his northern advance. He had, as so often, divided his armoured strength but Major General Gustav von Vaerst's 15th Panzer Division engaged 1st Armoured Division south of Msus, inflicted further losses of men and equipment, and compelled Messervy to fall back to Charruba, some 40 miles north of Msus and 70 miles east of Benghazi. On learning of this, Godwin-Austen instructed Messervy to retire to Mechili and Tuker to order 7th Indian Brigade out of Benghazi to make for Mechili as well.

To Auchinleck, no doubt with the prospect of Churchill's wrath in mind, the thought of abandoning Benghazi was dreadful. He therefore 'advised' Ritchie to cancel Godwin-Austen's orders. Ritchie duly complied – he could hardly have done otherwise – and on being faced with strong objections from Godwin-Austen, who in turn was supported by Messervy and Tuker, the army commander took 4th Indian Division under his own direct command to ensure that Auchinleck's requirements were met.

The new orders were clearly designed to satisfy a suggestion by Churchill that 4th Indian Division should hold out at Benghazi. They gave instructions that 4th Indian Division – which in practice meant 7th Indian Brigade – should indeed hold out at Benghazi, while 1st Armoured Division guarded its left flank by blocking any Axis advance from Msus. The 7th Indian Brigade was also ordered to threaten Rommel's communications by striking south-east towards Antelat. For this purpose, as Auchinleck announced enthusiastically to his staff, it would be split up into 'small mobile columns with artillery'. Auchinleck's interference, declares Captain Liddell Hart, merely 'resulted in the British becoming spread out and static in trying to cover the 140 miles stretch between Benghazi and Mechili, while Rommel from his central position at Msus, was allowed time and freedom to develop his action, as well as a choice of alternative objectives.'

On the 27th, Rommel took full advantage of the situation. His Afrika Korps moved towards Mechili but only as a diversion to distract attention from his true objective: Benghazi. By a cruel irony, bad weather that had hampered the Desert Air Force throughout Rommel's offensive allowed only one Axis movement to be spotted from the air: this feint by the Afrika Korps. Messervy headed off to counter it and so was unable to give any assistance to Tuker.

Three Axis formations now closed in on Benghazi: 90th Light thrust north along the Via Balbia; on its right flank the Italian XX Corps struck north from Antelat; still further to the east the Marcks Group, accompanied by Rommel in person, raced north-west from Msus. The 7th Indian Brigade, separated into the 'mobile columns' so favoured by Auchinleck, was in no position to resist these converging attacks. During the 28th, it became clear that Benghazi could not be held and was in grave danger of being isolated. Tuker therefore asked permission to evacuate the port and received reluctant permission from Eighth Army headquarters. Tuker's own headquarters managed to escape up the coastal road but before the bulk of 7th Indian Brigade could follow, the road was blocked by the Marcks Group that had swept round east of Benghazi. Brigadier Harold Briggs therefore turned back and struck out to the south-east over the open desert. He evaded his enemies and reached Mechili with very few casualties.

Rommel personally entered Benghazi on the morning of 29 January, though he must have been disappointed to discover that it would be useless as a port for quite some time. The Germans had carried out extensive demolitions before evacuating it after CRUSADER and Briggs had organized further destruction prior to his departure on the previous day. The harbour facilities had been thoroughly wrecked and the harbour itself was heavily mined and littered with sunken vessels. Indeed, although Rommel's daring counterstroke had certainly ruined ACROBAT and humiliated the British, he had as yet captured no territory of real strategic importance.

Nor did it seem likely that he would do so. The momentum of his attack was petering out and his supplies, particularly of petrol, were running dangerously low. Though he sent small mobile forces eastward to alarm and confuse his opponents, the bulk of the German armour was compelled to remain in Msus and the bulk of the German infantry in Benghazi. For their part, Auchinleck and Ritchie, aware that further retirements would hand Rommel a vital strategic prize, were anxious not to yield any more ground if this could be avoided.

Sadly, while it might well have been possible for XIII Corps to have held firm had it retired to and consolidated its strength around Mechili earlier, as its commander had wished, its formations were now both disorganized and disheartened. Neither Godwin-Austen nor Messervy nor Tuker had any confidence in their ability to resist further pressure. In their view, there was no alternative to a withdrawal of all Eighth Army units to the new defences being prepared at and south of Gazala; this would also have the advantage of reducing the length of the supply line from Eighth Army's base at Tobruk. On 4 February, their superiors reluctantly agreed and XIII Corps, followed but not pressed by Rommel, fell back to the Gazala Line which it had reached and occupied by the 6th.

There was no attempt at a counter-attack as the higher command had hoped and the campaign ended tamely. The first week of February 1942 had seen Britain suffer two heavy blows: one strategic, the other psychological. The effects of the former would quickly become apparent and will be dealt with later; the consequences of the latter were less obvious at first but would prove just as harmful and just as long-lasting. They may be described collectively as a loss of trust.

For everyone in Eighth Army, this ignominious repulse wiped out all satisfaction felt over the undoubted success of CRUSADER. As men tried to assess the causes of this abrupt reversal of fortunes, there developed an unhealthy admiration for the enemy general who, as the German historian Paul Carell proudly notes in *The Foxes of the Desert*, became for both sides 'the personification of the bold ruse, the lightning attack, the wild chase across the desert'. As Auchinleck recognized, there was 'very real danger' that Rommel might become 'a kind of magician or bogey-man to our troops'. Unhappily, the only way in which he tried to mitigate this was to demand that Rommel's name was not to be mentioned and Eighth Army should refer only to 'the Germans', 'the Axis powers' or 'the enemy'. They were orders that would prove as ineffective as they were pathetic.

One reason for the exaggerated praise heaped on Rommel was that his soldiers knew and his enemies seem to have instinctively realized that he was always in complete control of the forces under him. This knowledge emphasized the concern felt in Eighth Army over the way in which its own activities were being directed.

It will be recalled that Ritchie had agreed, if reluctantly, to the initial retirement desired by Godwin-Austen and his divisional commanders, but had been overridden by Auchinleck. 'It is now clear,' states Field Marshal Carver, 'that it was Auchinleck's intervention that caused the counter-order that led to disorder.' On later occasions, Ritchie would assess Rommel's intentions more accurately than did Auchinleck and Carver feels that Ritchie should 'have demanded either that he should be allowed freedom to command his army in his own way, or be replaced. But he was too decent, loyal and traditional a soldier to put his superior, whom he liked and admired, in such a difficult position. He was to suffer for it.'

He was indeed, both during the war and after it. He continued to receive instructions that, says General Sir William Jackson in *The North African Campaign 1940-43*, were 'passed on to him by Auchinleck in a voluminous shower of letters and signals', and despite his own justified doubts, he continued to carry them out. Yet Auchinleck allowed his official biographer, John Connell, to place all responsibility for Eighth Army's defeats onto Ritchie and when Ritchie protested, 'made it quite clear that he would do nothing to support or help me.' Since Connell had omitted vital documents in whole or in part, misdated signals and indulged in every kind of innuendo, Ritchie was surely justified in claiming that Auchinleck 'did to me what I consider a dishonourable and disloyal thing'.[5]

It was particularly dishonourable since during the period of his command of Eighth Army, it was Ritchie's own loyalty to Auchinleck that had virtually forfeited his own independence. This in turn had led to difficulties with his corps commanders who saw that Eighth Army was really being controlled from Cairo, an arrangement that they regarded as disadvantageous and dangerous.

Lieutenant General Willoughby Norrie is dismissed, rather slightingly, in most accounts as brave, charming but somewhat indecisive. This judgement fails to give him the credit he frequently deserved for assessing a situation more accurately than his superiors and he had already observed the ill effects of Auchinleck imposing his wishes on an inexperienced army commander. At the start of CRUSADER, Norrie had questioned the principal objectives and the detailed responsibilities of individual units laid down in the plan prepared by Auchinleck. His suggestions had been overruled. Later in that battle, Norrie had protested against orders sent from Ritchie on the 'advice' of Auchinleck that he felt meant he must conform 'to every movement of Rommel's'; what a later Eighth Army commander would call 'dancing to Rommel's tune'. Again he was disregarded. Norrie had taken no part in the fighting in January 1942, but it had done nothing to make him alter his doubts about the way in which Eighth Army was being commanded.

Norrie's fellow corps commander, Lieutenant General Godwin-Austen, had been very much involved in the fighting in January 1942 and he was most unhappy that his instructions had first been approved by Ritchie and then countermanded on the insistence of Auchinleck. He was still more disgusted by orders having been given directly from Army HQ to a commander of one of his subordinate divisions. He therefore offered his resignation, which Ritchie accepted after receiving Auchinleck's permission. Godwin-Austen was replaced by Lieutenant General William 'Strafer' Gott, who had commanded 7th Armoured Division during CRUSADER. He shared Norrie's views on the subject of Eighth Army being directed from Cairo and since he was a stronger character, he expressed his concerns much more forcefully.

With Gott and Norrie, in Field Marshal Carver's expressive phrase, 'ganging up against' Ritchie as being just Auchinleck's 'mouthpiece', it was perhaps inevitable that some divisional commanders should follow their example. Messervy was especially unhappy about the orders and counter-orders of Auchinleck and Ritchie; Tuker turned to poetry to condemn the higher command for making 'the same silly mistakes'. The leaders of the divisions from Australia, New Zealand and South Africa, perhaps more independently-minded by nature and with responsibilities to their own governments to consider, also made their disquiet abundantly clear.

By the time active operations in the desert resumed with an assault by Rommel on the Gazala Line in May 1942, this 'indiscipline at the top' as General Fraser calls it was widespread. 'Orders,' says Fraser, 'were received, doubted, questioned, discussed.' Indeed, with formation commanders querying the decisions of their superiors, the army commander passing on instructions that he correctly believed to be wrong, and the C-in-C giving guidance from afar and then only after lengthy staff meetings that, according to de Guingand who had to endure them, 'used to go on sometimes for hours' by which time the situation at the front had often changed dramatically, it may well be asked who was really directing Eighth Army? The only proper answer would appear to be 'No-one'.

Nor did lack of confidence flow in only one direction. Rommel's counter-offensive in January 1942 had caused an outburst from General Auchinleck. In messages to London and to his staff, he denounced not only the leaders but the men of the armoured formations. They were, he claimed, unable 'to compete with the enemy satisfactorily', or to resist him 'for any length of time', or to meet him 'in the open, even when superior to him in numbers'. As for the advanced infantry units, they had been 'disconcerted' by Rommel's attack and too easily 'pushed aside'. Certainly the whole episode had been an inglorious one, but it might be recalled that it was Auchinleck's decisions that had placed inexperienced units in dangerously over-extended positions, had weakened the infantry formations still further by dividing them into Jock Columns and had made a bad situation worse by refusing to allow an organized retirement. It does seem, therefore, that he might have been less scathing in his comments regarding others.

Attributing blame, unfortunately, became common practice in Eighth Army. Few units doubted their own abilities, so it was perhaps only natural that they should transfer the responsibility for defeat onto other formations or other branches of the army. This lack of trust brought with it a growing cynicism that ate away at the army's unity and was further increased by the realization that the sequence of ebb and flow, of victory followed by defeat, had all happened before. It became known by a number of sardonic expressions: 'The Annual Swan up the Desert', 'The Gazala Gallop', 'The Benghazi Handicap', 'The Djebel Stakes'.[6] The haunting fear grew that success would never last, that victory would never be permanent, and that Eighth Army was doomed to fight up and down the Western Desert for all time. It was a chilling prospect.

Nor were Eighth Army's problems hidden from the enemy. Having cracked the American diplomatic code, the Axis powers could read the reports of the US military attaché in Cairo, Major Bonner Fellers, to his superiors in Washington. This breach of security lasted from the autumn of 1941 to late June 1942, when it was revealed to the Allies by Ultra. The 'Fellers Intercepts', if we may so call them, then ceased abruptly and their existence only became public knowledge in 1966 when they were revealed by David Kahn, a member of the American Cryptogram Association, in a comprehensive work entitled *The Code Breakers*.

Understandably elated by his scoop and perhaps misled by the German name for the Fellers Intercepts being 'The Good Source', Kahn declared that: 'They provided Rommel with undoubtedly the broadest and clearest picture of enemy forces and intentions available to any Axis commander throughout the whole war.' It was a judgement eagerly seized upon and further exaggerated by those desperate to find an excuse for British failures in North Africa, by whom it has been proclaimed that Eighth Army was thus placed under 'a fatal handicap'.

If this was the case, it does seem surprising that Eighth Army's most disgraceful defeats should have taken place in July 1942, after the 'fatal handicap' had been removed. However, in fact it is clear that for none of the major battles fought during the period when they were being read did the Fellers Intercepts really provide Rommel with accurate information of Eighth Army's intentions.

At the time of CRUSADER, for instance, Rommel knew so little of his opponents' plans that, far from making ready to resist Eighth Army's assault, he was preparing an attack of his own on Tobruk. He had personally gone to a conference in Rome and flew back to North Africa, via Athens, only just before the battle began on 18 November 1941, and then he believed at first that it was only a reconnaissance in force. Similarly, when organizing his attack of 21 January 1942, Rommel was concerned, as he wrote to his wife on the 20th, that the British might attack him first. Had he any knowledge of British plans, he would have been aware that no such operation was envisaged before mid–February.

Nor did the Fellers Intercepts ever give Rommel a full knowledge of the Eighth Army Order of Battle or the location of its units, as is confirmed by Rommel's Chief Intelligence Officer, Lieutenant Colonel (later Major General) Friedrich Wilhelm, Freiherr von Mellenthin, in his book *Panzer Battles.* He tells us that in January 1942, information on XXX Corps was 'far from clear'; he knew only that it was not in the forward area. He believed the forward units and those at Agedabia were parts of 4th Indian Division, whereas they were really under 1st Armoured. He believed the bulk of 4th Indian was at Benghazi, whereas only one of its brigades was there. He believed 1st Armoured's tanks were at Agedabia, whereas one of its armoured brigades was some 30 miles away at Antelat and the other far back at Tobruk.

Von Mellenthin also admits that prior to their attack on the Gazala Line in May 1942, the Germans were unaware of the numbers and dispositions of Eighth Army's infantry or armoured units, the existence of fortified positions and the extent of the British minefields. He adds that it may have been fortunate that 'we underestimated the British strength, for had we known the full facts even Rommel might have balked at an attack on such a greatly superior enemy.'

The Fellers Intercepts, then, did not give Rommel a decisive strategic advantage, and they clearly gave him no decisive tactical advantage either. When Fellers had acquired his information, he would first draft his message. It then had to be encoded, a task that was not treated as a matter of much urgency. Then the message had to be sent off – David Kahn says by the Egyptian Telegraph Company in Cairo – thus imposing more delay.

After the message had been sent and intercepted, it had to be decoded and translated. Any gaps in it had to be filled and the message put into the German code and dispatched to Rommel's Intelligence staff. This inevitably took time. Kahn does quote an instance of a signal reaching Rommel only three-and-a-half hours after its interception, but since he also states that Fellers had drafted the message on the day before it was transmitted, the period that had elapsed since Fellers had first gained his knowledge was really considerably longer. In any case, in the desert a great deal could happen, even in three-and-a-half hours.

Moreover, even at the time when Fellers did first acquire his information, it was usually already out of date. On 1 June, for example, Fellers reported the progress of the Battle of Gazala up to 30 May, but Rommel was already aware of what had happened at least two days earlier. During Rommel's January offensive, a Fellers Intercept on the 29th purported to give details of the strength and location of the British armour, but these were no longer accurate after the previous hard fighting and in any event were of no use to Rommel who had already decided he could not move eastward in strength after taking Benghazi. Another Fellers Intercept on 6 February revealed that the British were digging in at and around Gazala, but Rommel had been told of this already by his mobile units.

Indeed we know from von Mellenthin and also from Hans-Otto Behrendt, a former lieutenant on Panzerarmee Afrika's Intelligence staff, in his book *Rommel's Intelligence in the Desert Campaign*, that Rommel had a far better source of information than the Fellers Intercepts. This was his Wireless Interception Section led by the brilliant Captain Alfred Seebohm that read the signals passing between the various Eighth Army formations; they were normally in plain English, for British wireless discipline was notoriously poor. It was his Interception Section that gave Rommel any information that he did have about the positions of British units prior to his offensive on 21 January and in particular that they had been dispersed. Even then Rommel was not fully convinced until the dispersal was confirmed by his Chief Operations Officer, Lieutenant Colonel Siegfried Westphal, who had been taken over the front line in a reconnaissance aircraft.

During the course of the fighting, it was again not the Fellers Intercepts but his Interception Section that informed Rommel of the activities of Eighth Army and did so, moreover, not after a lapse of hours but almost immediately. Seebohm stayed in close contact with Rommel and often parked his vehicle next to that of his general. It is said that he sometimes handed Rommel translations of messages picked up by his unit before their intended recipients had sent a formal acknowledgement. When the Wireless Interception Section was overrun by an Australian attack on 10 July, Behrendt describes it as a 'catastrophe' with 'more serious consequences for Panzerarmee Afrika' than the earlier loss of 'the Good Source'.

To this it can be added that both Behrendt and Ronald Lewin in his *Rommel as Military Commander* give their opinion that Rommel relied chiefly on his instincts and his 'feel' for a battlefield and Intelligence of all kinds affected his planning 'less than might be supposed'. To claim that the Fellers Intercepts placed Eighth Army under 'a fatal handicap' is therefore absurd. Yet in one field they did give Rommel useful information that he could not have gained from any other source: an insight into what was happening well behind the battle lines.

Bonner Fellers had little respect and perhaps little liking for the British. His reports were invariably critical of their performance and pessimistic about their prospects and he delighted in recounting the disagreements that sometimes surfaced and the outbursts of alarm and anxiety that occasionally convulsed Cairo. A knowledge of the unhappiness and falling morale in the British ranks must often have lifted Rommel's own somewhat mercurial spirits.

Rommel must also have been heartened to discover that the British still thought his tanks were superior; this was quite untrue but it meant that his enemies had not fathomed the real reasons for the panzers' successes, let alone discovered ways of defeating them. He must have been encouraged to learn that Fellers was contemptuous of British leadership. His satisfaction would have been all the greater because he had shrewdly deduced, as he said in a letter to his wife on 14 January, that the British would 'look all the more for victories in North Africa' to offset their disasters in the Far East.

In fact, if the Germans had only had an equivalent to the Ultra Intelligence that enabled them to read the signals passing between London and Cairo, Rommel's pleasure would have been complete, for he would have seen that British lack of trust and confidence was more widespread than he had realized. General Auchinleck might blame poor equipment and the men in the ranks for the setbacks in the desert, but others held very different views.

In November 1941, General Sir Alan Brooke had become Chief of the Imperial General Staff. He was a much stronger and sterner figure than Dill and on 30 January 1942, he noted in his diary that the success of Rommel's counter-offensive showed 'Nothing less than bad generalship on the part of Auchinleck'. Churchill was equally unimpressed by the way Auchinleck had handled the incident. When he wrote about it six years after the war,[7] he complained bitterly of the way in which all the initiative had been left to Rommel, considered but rejected the excuses put forward by Auchinleck in his Official Despatch, and concluded by urging that 'the British nation' should not be 'misled into thinking that the technical inferiority of our tanks was the only reason for this considerable and far-reaching reverse'.

The obvious doubts that Churchill and Brooke entertained of Auchinleck's abilities were made apparent in signals that became ever more unkind. These ruined Auchinleck's own morale and self-confidence until, as de Guingand laments, he became reluctant ever to reach any 'definite decision'. They also made him increasingly resentful, and by early May relations between London and Cairo were deplorable. It would have delighted Rommel still more to have known that the main cause of this breakdown in trust had been the strategic success that he had gained in February 1942.

One of the towns in Cyrenaica that the British retreat in February had abandoned to Rommel was the lovely little port of Derna, resting between steep hills and a bright blue sea. Alan Moorehead calls it 'a green pool of colour in the desert' and all accounts talk with pleasure of its neat snow-white houses with their cool shaded courts, its palm trees, banana plantations, pomegranate groves, lush vegetable gardens and purple bougainvillaea. However, it was not the loss of such delightful sights that was so disastrous for the British.

Just south of Derna there was a great complex of airfields at Martuba. These, naturally, were lost as well and on 7 February became the base of Axis warplanes that would make good use of them in the future. Even more grievous, as it would transpire, was the fact that they could of course no longer be used by the Desert Air Force.

Notes

1. *The Mediterranean and Middle East* Volume III (September 1941 to September 1942) *British Fortunes reach their Lowest Ebb* by Major General I.S.O. Playfair with Captain F.C. Flynn RN, Brigadier C.J.C. Molony and Group Captain T.P. Gleave.
2. Campbell was promoted to major general after the battle. He was killed on 5 March 1942 when his staff car overturned on a road recently repaired with wet clay that had not had time to harden.
3. Full details of the Allied and Axis tanks can be found in the *Official History*, which has provided the main source for the facts set out herein.
4. 'I' stood for 'Infantry', with whom the British heavy tanks were trained to co-operate.
5. It is pleasant to record that Field Marshal Carver, who served not only in Eighth Army but in XII Corps which Ritchie ably commanded in the campaign in North-West Europe, wrote his *Dilemmas of the Desert War* partly to defend Ritchie's reputation. In his book, Carver examines Connell's misrepresentations in considerable detail, and exposes them!
6. The Djebel Akhdar or Green Mountains lay in the Cyrenaican 'Bulge' between Benghazi and Derna. It was 3,000 feet high and had fertile valleys with a reddish soil that reminded many an Englishman of Devonshire.
7. In his *The Second World War*, Volume IV, *The Hinge of Fate*.

Chapter 3

Shadow over Malta

Rommel's counterstroke had shaken the confidence of Eighth Army but not that of the Desert Air Force. The soldiers felt humiliated but the airmen could look back on the episode with some satisfaction, the more so since they could so easily have suffered a disaster early on. As the Germans raced towards Antelat on 22 January, its aerodrome was almost entirely waterlogged. Yet the ground crews managed to manhandle their warplanes to the only area from which they could take off and all were airborne just in time, apart from two Hurricanes and four Kittyhawks awaiting repair after previous damage; these, of course, were destroyed and prevented from falling into enemy hands.

Thereafter, the Desert Air Force was not slow to make its presence felt. On 24 January, the Hurricanes of 274 Squadron shot down four Junkers Ju 87 Stuka dive-bombers plus three of their escorting fighters for the loss of one of their own number that crash-landed. There was little further interference from the Axis airmen and the Desert Air Force's Hurricanes, Tomahawks and Kittyhawks turned their attention to strafing Axis vehicles, destroying or damaging some 120 on 26 January and about 100 more on 5 February. After the fighting on land had died down, the Allied airmen continued to clash with the enemy air forces and on 14 February, the Kittyhawks of 112 Squadron RAF and 3 Squadron RAAF claimed to have shot down twenty Italian aircraft without loss. Sadly, though, in February 1942 no aspect of Britain's war effort would enjoy success for very long.

Probably the best-known pilot in the Desert Air Force at this time was Squadron Leader Ernest Michelson Mason. Having completed his flying training in Egypt, he had originally been posted to a bomber squadron but as this was not to his taste, he arranged an exchange of postings with another pilot that took him to 80 Squadron, a fighter unit then equipped with Gladiators. After Italy's declaration of war, No. 80 acquired a flight of Hurricanes, one of which was flown by Mason. In August 1940, the members of this flight all left to help form a new Hurricane squadron, No. 274. This saw constant action during the first British conquest of Cyrenaica and by the end of January 1941, Pilot Officer Mason had become the RAF's top-scoring 'ace' in the desert, with a total of thirteen enemy aircraft shot down, not counting some 'shared' successes. He had also received a Distinguished Flying Cross, an award made far more rarely to pilots in the Middle East than to those stationed in Britain, and his fame was increased by his having been supposed, though incorrectly, to have shot down Major Ernesto Botto, an Italian ace of the Spanish Civil War.

Mason had also become well-known for other reasons. He had grown a heavy black beard, an adornment fairly common in the Fleet Air Arm but at this time reportedly the only one in the RAF. He had been given the nickname of 'Imshi', Arabic for 'go away' or 'scram'; 'a word,' according to Richard Townshend Bickers in *The Desert Air War 1939–1945*, 'to which he resorted with vehemence when importuned by vagrants, pedlars, pimps and other undesirables.' He also enlivened the atmosphere of his squadron by his fondness for driving either a large motorcycle or a captured Italian light tank round its aerodrome. When less aggressively inclined, he would regale his colleagues with tunes on a saxophone, an instrument on which he was a highly-accomplished performer.

So far, Mason had only met Italian aircraft but the capture of airfields in Cyrenaica made it possible to fly Hurricanes from these to Malta to reinforce 261 Squadron, then conducting the defence of the island fortress. A flight from 274 Squadron led by Mason, now a flying officer and soon to be appointed flight lieutenant, duly set off for Malta on 18 March 1941. On 13 April Mason fearlessly, if rashly, attacked four Messerschmitt Bf [1] 109s single-handed. He fired on one of these that may have been destroyed; it is not logged in

German records but witnesses confirmed that two aircraft had gone into the sea. The second of these was Mason's Hurricane which he had to 'ditch' after being counter-attacked by the remaining 109s. He was later evacuated to Egypt with a bullet wound in his right hand, a broken nose caused by having hit his fighter's windscreen and, judging from photographs taken at the time, no beard, having presumably shaved it off.

In July, Mason became a squadron leader and took charge of No. 261, now re-formed in Iraq. In August, the squadron took part in a joint British-Russian advance into Iran (or Persia to those such as Churchill who preferred that older name) designed to secure a route by which supplies could be sent to Britain's new ally. There was only one recorded combat, when Squadron Leader Mason shot down an elderly Hawker Audax biplane on the 26th. This comparative lack of action did not appeal to him and he was delighted when on 8 January 1942 he was sent back to the Western Desert to take command of 94 Squadron, which on 14 February moved to Gambut airfield, south-east of Tobruk, to begin operations. There was just one flaw. Soon after Mason joined the squadron, it converted from Hurricanes to Kittyhawks. Neither he nor his men had any experience on this type and February 1942 was not a good time for an inexperienced unit to see combat.

During his earlier service in the desert, 'Imshi' Mason had often strafed enemy aerodromes, sharing in the destruction of a number of machines, variously estimated at from thirteen to nineteen, on the ground. On 15 February he led eight of No. 94's Kittyhawks in an attack on the Martuba airfields. This appears to have done little damage and as the British pilots turned for home, they were pounced upon by a Messerschmitt Bf 109 flown by *Oberfeldwebel* (Flight Sergeant) Otto Schulz that had hastily taken off from Martuba. In their *Fighters over the Desert*, Christopher Shores and Hans Ring state that 'no evasive action was taken by the British pilots' and Schulz believed they were 'novices under an instructional flight'. In quick succession he shot down four of them: Mason, Pilot Officer Marshall, Sergeant Belcher and Sergeant Weightman were all killed.

It was not at first known what had happened to Mason and he was reported missing. On the 25th, an army patrol found his body and buried it. For the Desert Air Force the death of such a successful, colourful and popular pilot was, say Shores and Ring, 'a particularly great loss'. Otto Schulz, naturally, was elated by his achievement, the more so since he believed he had later shot down a fifth Kittyhawk that had in fact returned to base badly damaged and with a wounded pilot. Shores and Ring report that Schulz's 'fellow pilots made a large tin-plate Knights' Cross replica, which they ceremoniously presented to him next morning. A few days later Field Marshal Kesselring arrived at the airfield to present the genuine article.'[2]

Field Marshal Albert Kesselring, a soldier turned airman who later in Italy would turn soldier again, like all good leaders knew the value of decorations and greatly enjoyed presenting them. In February 1942, however, his main attention was directed towards the most important focal point of the Desert War and this, by an odd paradox, lay outside the desert.

While supply lines in the desert were of immense importance, supply lines to the desert were of equal significance. Since the Axis powers dominated the Mediterranean, British convoys to the Middle East had to steam some 14,000 miles, all the way round the Cape of Good Hope. On the other hand, Axis convoys had to cross only 350 miles of sea from the port of Messina in the north of Sicily to the port of Tripoli in North Africa.

Fortunately, this was not the whole story. Just 60 miles south of Sicily, right in the path of the Axis supply routes, lay the island fortress of Malta. From this, aircraft, submarines and surface warships could and did decimate the Axis convoys. 'It requires no hindsight,' declares Ronald Lewin in *The Life and Death of the Afrika Korps*, 'to observe that for both sides Malta was the key to a sound strategic posture in the Mediterranean.'

This was certainly realized by Admiral Sir Andrew Browne Cunningham, Commander-in-Chief of the Mediterranean Fleet, who in the face of a general opinion that the Italian entry into the war made the island untenable insisted that 'Malta should be held at all costs'. It was also realized by Churchill, who on 2 August 1940 was responsible for the beautifully-named Operation HURRY that saw the first occasion on which Hurricane fighters were flown off aircraft carriers to reinforce the island's defences. It was certainly not

realized by General Sir Claude Auchinleck, the chief beneficiary of
Malta's activities.

Yet in August 1941, soon after Auchinleck had been appointed C-
in-C, Middle East, Churchill had gleefully informed him that
attacks from Malta would cause untold difficulties for the
maintenance of Rommel's army. If Auchinleck doubted the prime
minister's assurances, as it seems he did, the events of the next few
months should surely have been enough to convince him. In
September, Malta's striking forces sent 28 per cent of all supplies
destined for Rommel to the bottom. In October, the proportion was
21 per cent. In November, the month when CRUSADER began, it
was as much as 63 per cent. Nor were Malta's attacks limited to anti-
shipping raids. On the night of 21/22 October, for example,
bombers based on the island hit the oil storage depot at Naples,
starting fires that their crews said were the biggest they had ever
seen.

None of these facts would alter Auchinleck's opinions. Churchill
and Brooke were well aware, as the latter subsequently noted in his
diary, that Auchinleck 'entirely failed' to understand Malta's
importance. Their knowledge played a major part in the dispatch of
those harsh signals that so upset Auchinleck and soured the relations
between London and Cairo. They did not, unfortunately, overcome
Auchinleck's obstinate indifference to Malta's fate. As late as August
1942, when the island had been brought very close to surrender, the
C-in-C, Middle East would refuse to stage a diversionary attack to
entice attention away from a convoy attempting to go to its aid.
Malta's retention, he stated, was not absolutely necessary to his
plans.

Auchinleck's lack of strategic vision would have mattered less if
his enemies had shared it. Tragically, Malta's value was obvious not
only to Churchill, Cunningham and Brooke: Hitler, Kesselring and
Rommel appreciated it as well. The Führer's estimation of Malta's
importance was such that on 2 December 1941 he deprived his
soldiers on the Moscow front of the assistance of Fliegerkorps II,
transferring it to Sicily. Here it joined up with Fliegerkorps X
stationed in the Balkans to form Luftflotte (Air Fleet) 2. To control
this, Field Marshal Kesselring was also ordered to leave Russia and

to proceed to Rome where he was soon to be appointed C-in-C, South with authority over all German naval and air forces in the Mediterranean; this added the Luftwaffe units in North Africa and in practice Italy's Regia Aeronautica as well to those under his command.

In all, Kesselring could call on 2,000 warplanes and had been given precise orders by Hitler as to how to use them. He was to 'ensure safe lines of communication' with North Africa. 'In this connection,' Hitler correctly considered, 'the suppression of Malta' by attacks both on the island and on the convoys bringing it supplies was 'particularly important'.

On 22 December Kesselring, who shared his Führer's views, set out to suppress Malta. During the last week of 1941, more than 200 aircraft attacked the island. In January 1942 the tempo increased, with over 100 raids dropping more than 1,800 tons of bombs. The handful of RAF Hurricanes that formed the fighter defence inflicted casualties and limited the amount of damage caused but they were heavily outnumbered and by the end of the month, only twenty-eight of them remained serviceable. Worse still, as Malta was increasingly forced onto the defensive, so her attacks on the Axis convoy routes fell away. Rommel at last began to receive supplies and reinforcements and it was their arrival that was one of the factors that encouraged his daring counterstroke against Eighth Army.

Persistent heavy rain provided Malta with a merciful relief from her ordeal for the first week in February but as soon as the weather improved, the previous pattern was resumed. Kesselring's men renewed their assault on the island, while Malta's striking forces, despite gallant efforts, were able to impose only a minor restriction on the amount of Axis supplies reaching North Africa.

Malta's surface warships, in fact, were unable to cause any interference with the enemy's supply routes and they themselves received unpleasant attention from the Luftwaffe. On the morning of 11 February, light cruiser *Cleopatra* and destroyer *Fortune* were attacked north of Malta. The raiders were engaged by Hurricanes which, without loss, shot down a Messerschmitt Bf 109 and a Junkers Ju 88 bomber and so damaged another Ju 88 that it crash-landed in Sicily. They were not, however, able to prevent *Cleopatra* suffering damage and casualties from a very near miss. The destroyer, as befitted her name, was more fortunate.

That night, a raid on Grand Harbour by Junkers Ju 88s ended the career of a less lucky destroyer. A bomb crashed into the engine-room of HMS *Maori*, starting a raging fire. Happily, most of her crew had gone ashore and the hit killed only one of the watchkeepers, injuring eight others; splinters killed two more men and injured six on destroyer *Decoy* moored nearby. Also close at hand was the liner *Ajax* and she was able to lower her boats and rescue *Maori*'s survivors. *Maori*'s fires, however, could not be mastered and two hours later she blew up.

Malta's aircraft and submarines did attack Axis transports during February and sank a small number but at a heavy cost. On the 4th, six Blenheims of 21 Squadron, ordered to bomb enemy vessels in the harbour of Palermo, Sicily, failed to locate them, attacked targets on land instead and lost four aircraft, three being downed by anti-aircraft guns and the fourth crashing into the sea when its wing-tip accidentally hit the water as it made a tight turn. Only one member of the four crews survived and among the dead was the CO, Wing Commander William Selkirk. Two days later, three more of No. 21's Blenheims, now led by a New Zealander, Squadron Leader Russell Stewart, were searching for Axis shipping off North Africa when they were intercepted by 109s. All three were shot down and this time there were no survivors at all.

Nor were aircraft the only casualties. Friday, 13 February proved tragically unlucky for HM Submarine *Tempest*, one of three from Malta that were patrolling the convoy routes looking for targets. Unfortunately, it was *Tempest* that was spotted, by the Italian torpedo-boat *Circe*, a dangerous opponent for she had previously assisted in the sinking of two other British submarines: *Grampus* in June 1940 and *Union* in July 1941. Repeated attacks with depth-charges forced the badly-damaged *Tempest* to the surface, to sink shortly afterwards with the loss of thirty-nine of her crew.

In this dreadful month, even British successes seemed fated to leave a bitter taste. The other 'subs' on patrol with *Tempest* were *Upright* and *Una*, and on the day before her loss, both sighted the Italian tanker *Lucania*. Richard Woodman in his *Malta Convoys* relates that on this and previous occasions, *Lucania* 'had been granted immunity from attack' since the fuel she carried was to be supplied to 'ships repatriating civilians from East Africa'. *Upright* therefore refrained from attacking her but *Una* was less forbearing and sank her.

It is not clear whether *Una* had received no warning of *Lucania*'s immunity or whether Lieutenant Martin, the submarine's commander, had simply mistaken his target's identity. It is quite clear that the Italians were understandably displeased: Count Galeazzo Ciano, Mussolini's foreign minister and son-in-law, noted in his diary that the British had broken their word without any justification. It should be emphasized that the British government was horrified by what had happened and Woodman tells us that 'Martin was flown home and had to explain his actions personally to the Foreign Secretary, Anthony Eden.' Since his career was not affected, presumably it was accepted that he was not to blame for the incident. However, it was hardly one in which the Royal Navy could take much satisfaction.

Another unfortunate episode took place late on the same Friday the 13th that had already seen the loss of *Tempest*. This one was even more galling since at first glance it appeared an admirable example of the determination and persistence of Malta's striking forces. A reconnaissance Maryland had sighted a small convoy south-west of the island and a flight of Albacore torpedo-planes[3] was sent out to engage it. They succeeded in putting a torpedo into the Italian freighter *Ariosto* that left her on fire and dead in the water. In the early hours of the 14th another of Malta's submarines, the *P38*, sighted the crippled vessel and finished her off. It would later transpire that *Ariosto* had been transferring British prisoners of war to Italy and large numbers of them were among the 158 men who died when she went down.

Worse still, for all their efforts, Malta's striking forces were not able to disrupt the Axis powers' main effort in February to send supplies to Rommel. This was a plan to get two separate but closely co-ordinated convoys with a total of six merchantmen, guarded by a formidable number of warships, among them the battleship *Caio Duilio* and three cruisers, to Tripoli on the 24th of the month. The operation was revealed by Ultra and the British prepared their own plans to disrupt it. Eight submarines were sent to patrol off Tripoli and bombers and torpedo-planes from both Malta and the Middle East were warned to be ready to attack.

As might have been expected in February 1942, everything that could go wrong did go wrong. The enemy vessels were sighted during the night of the 21st/22nd by a radar-equipped Wellington, but its estimation of their position was very inaccurate and a flight of Albacores that was sent out naturally failed to find them. On the 22nd, the main effort was made by aircraft from North Africa but of the twenty-five machines that took off, only one bomber located its target and its attack was ineffectual. That night, a flight of Wellingtons from the Middle East attempted to find the Axis ships but only one did so (by accident) and its attack did no damage either. After dark on the 23rd, torpedo-bombers from Malta also sought out the enemy but again just one was able to make an attack and it was shot down by AA fire, the crew being killed.

Malta's submarines also achieved nothing. The only successful action was initiated by the redoubtable Italian torpedo-boat *Circe* when on 23 February she detected *P38*, the submarine that had sunk *Ariosto* earlier in the month, trying to reach a position from which she could launch her torpedoes against the supply ships. *Circe*'s depth-charges blew *P38* to the surface, where the destroyer *Usodimare*, racing onto the scene, opened fire on her. Some shells clearly struck home, for *P38*'s bow reared out of the water and she sank stern-first. An underwater explosion followed, leaving the sea fouled with wreckage and the gruesome remains of the submarine's crew. Woodman relates that *Circe* picked up a canvas bag containing 'two black flags and three Union jacks'. By the 24th all the Axis merchantmen had reached Tripoli safely.

The main reason why Malta's bombers and torpedo-planes had so little success during February was the constant assaults on the island made by Kesselring's men.[4] A large proportion of these were directed against the airfields and their facilities. With workshops reduced to wreckage and runways cratered again and again, the ground crews toiled heroically to keep the various warplanes serviceable, only to see them destroyed by later raids. On 22

February, for instance, 37 Squadron had five of its Wellingtons put out of action by splinters and next day, when there were six raids altogether, two more Wellingtons were destroyed. This left the squadron with just one with which to attack the Axis supply ships at Tripoli. Piloted by Flying Officer Halliwell, it set off anyway; it was unable to find the enemy vessels, so bombed harbour installations instead.

Perhaps Malta's most harrowing day was 15 February when a series of raids kept the defenders on the alert literally all day, starting at 0800. Beaufighters flown by 252 Squadron destroyed an Italian float-plane but two of its own aircraft were shot down by Messerschmitt Bf 109s and a third damaged beyond repair on the ground. Two Marylands were also shot down by 109s and two Wellingtons wrecked on the ground by Junkers Ju 88s. One of the Ju 88s was downed by AA fire and two 109s in combats with Hurricanes, one of which also fell, leaving the number of Malta's single-engined fighters that were still serviceable at just eleven. The hardest blow fell in the evening when a raid by Ju 88s scored a bomb hit on a cinema, killing fifty-two servicemen and twenty-three civilians.

Under such pressure, it became increasingly difficult for Malta's striking forces to operate at all. As mentioned earlier, by the evening of 23 February, 37 Squadron was down to one serviceable Wellington. Furthermore, No. 37 had itself been a replacement for another Wellington squadron, No. 40, the remaining aircraft of which were withdrawn to Egypt on the 16th. No. 252, the misfortunes of whose Beaufighters on the previous day have already been recounted, also left for Egypt on the 16th, as did the Blenheims of the battered 21 Squadron on the 22nd.

By this time, the effects of strain, exhaustion and lack of sleep were also beginning to have a grave effect on all personnel. A vivid example of this would be seen on 24 February. Two Hurricanes from 249 Squadron were 'scrambled', flown by the Canadian Squadron Leader Stanley Turner, a very aggressive character with the unnerving habit of firing a large revolver in public, who had flown Hurricanes in the Battle of Britain with Douglas Bader's 242 Squadron, and Pilot Officer Donald Tedford, one of a number of

Americans on Malta who had joined the RAF as volunteers before the United States entered the war. Turner and Tedford were ordered to engage four enemy aircraft, but it appears that the flight controller confused the two plots recorded on his radar screen because he notified his pilots that their foes were immediately in front of them. In fact they were close behind, they were Messerschmitt Bf 109s and they caught the outnumbered Hurricanes completely by surprise.

There could only be one end to the brief fight that followed. Turner's Hurricane was hit in the engine and a fire started. Turner's cockpit had also been hit, so he was unable to bale out but mercifully he dived away so steeply that he blew out the flames and crash-landed with only minor injuries. Tedford was shot down and killed. It was thought, incorrectly, that he might have baled out into the sea and when the report reached Pilot Officer Howard Coffin, a member of another Hurricane squadron, No. 126, but a fellow American, he took off without orders to see if he could find any trace of Tedford. He would later record that: 'Nobody ever blamed me for leaving my post of duty.'

In addition to the losses of men and material caused by the air-raids, Malta was now suffering from a shortage of essential commodities. Equipment of all kinds, spare parts of all kinds, machine-gun bullets for the fighters, shells for the AA gunners, aviation fuel, kerosene – source of all heat and light on a small treeless island – and oil: all were becoming scarce. Most depressing of all was a shortage of food. Service personnel and civilians alike were being strictly rationed and items such as fresh vegetables were virtually unobtainable. Malta, in fact, was approaching a state of siege and there seemed little prospect of the siege being lifted in the near future.

It was for this reason that the loss of the Martuba airfields became so significant. If Malta was to survive, her needs would have to be met by running convoys to her. In theory, these could be sent from either Alexandria or Gibraltar. In February 1942, there was in practice only one choice available.

Convoys approaching Malta from the west had always suffered from the disadvantage that the majority of the escorting warships had to turn back when the dangerously restricted waters between

Sicily and Cape Bon, Tunisia, known as 'The Narrows', were reached. Moreover, the strength of Gibraltar's Force H had been gravely reduced by the loss of the aircraft carrier *Ark Royal* in November 1941, sunk by a U-boat shortly after she had flown off a batch of Hurricanes to reinforce Malta's defenders. Indeed, Force H was not even available in mid-February, having been recalled to the Clyde to provide cover for a big troop convoy leaving on the 16th for the long haul round the Cape of Good Hope. When Force H returned to Gibraltar on the 24th, the chiefs of staff would still expressly advise Admiral Cunningham that replenishing Malta from the west was not practicable.

On the other hand, in January 1942 a convoy from Alexandria had reached Malta successfully. This, though, was mainly because while passing through the waters between Crete and North Africa – an area soon to be known as 'Bomb Alley' – it had enjoyed the protection of fighters flying from British-held airfields in Cyrenaica rather than the attentions of Axis bombers flying from those same airfields.

This situation had now been reversed and no-one was more aware of it than Cunningham. On 7 February, he warned the chiefs of staff that the recent withdrawal of Eighth Army to Gazala had created a prospect of 'grim bleakness' for Malta. He confirmed his belief that 'if we could hold as far forward as Derna', it would be possible to supply Malta from Alexandria, but of course 'we are already behind that line'.

Nonetheless, Malta had to receive supplies and they could only come from the east, so Cunningham, no doubt with many misgivings, set about preparing to deliver them. His convoy, austerely known as MW9 instead of by a memorable code name as were many of the Malta convoys, consisted of three big fast freighters, suitably escorted, crammed with food, ammunition, aviation fuel in cans, motor vehicles and much other varied equipment. At the same time Cunningham planned to bring four empty supply ships that had remained at Malta since January back to Alexandria where they could be of further service. His hopes that their movement might also distract enemy attention from MW9, however, were not to be fulfilled.

Convoy MW9 left Alexandria in two sections on the evening of

12 February. The first group contained the merchantmen *Clan Campbell* and *Clan Chattan*, guarded by the anti-aircraft cruiser *Carlisle* and four destroyers; they were followed soon afterwards by the third merchantman, the *Rowallan Castle*, and four more destroyers. Early on the 13th, Rear Admiral Philip Vian also left Alexandria with three light cruisers and seven destroyers, the intention being that he would join the convoy on the morning of the 14th when it would no longer have the protection of British fighters from North Africa. The four empty ships, escorted by naval vessels based at Malta – light cruiser *Penelope* and six destroyers – left the island on the 13th as well and steamed eastward.

The Luftwaffe was also very active on the 13th. Hitler had ordered Kesselring to sink any supply ships making for Malta and Kesselring's airmen certainly did their best to obey their Führer's commands. They largely ignored the empty ships from Malta, but throughout the day they made repeated attacks on Convoy MW9. The merchantmen – slower, less well-armed and less well-protected than the warships – were naturally the principal targets, but their steadfast crews kept pushing doggedly on towards Malta. Mercifully, on this day it was possible for British fighter aircraft from North Africa to afford them some protection, while their escorts, at the cost of using up so much anti-aircraft ammunition that its use had to be rationed on the crucial day following, put up a daunting fire that helped to drive off raid after raid.

Not until the evening was the Luftwaffe's persistence rewarded, but then a Junkers Ju 88 broke through the AA barrage to score a direct hit on *Clan Campbell*. The bomb, smashing a huge hole in her deck, plunged into the engine-room and right through it to explode outside the ship. Heavily damaged and with her speed greatly reduced, she had no option but to turn back, escorted by a pair of destroyers. One of the vital supply ships would not now reach Malta.[5]

Night provided the convoy with a brief respite, but on 14 February the German assault was resumed. Rear Admiral Vian's ships had now increased the strength of the escort but the loss of the Martuba airfields exercised its baleful influence. The Allies' inability to use them meant that no fighters from Cyrenaica could help guard the convoy; the Axis possession of them meant that heavy attacks on it could be mounted from them. About midday, a Ju 88 hit *Clan Chattan* with a bomb that exploded in her after hold, bringing her to a halt, badly on fire. The ammunition that she carried started to explode and orders were given to abandon her. Destroyers rescued her crew, and then finished her off with torpedoes.

Shortly after *Clan Chattan* was hit, Convoy MW9 met the vessels from Malta. Vian now assumed the responsibility for escorting these to Alexandria, which task was achieved successfully, while *Penelope* and the destroyers from Malta took over the duty of guarding the last of the supply ships, *Rowallan Castle*. At about 1515, however, five Junkers Ju 88s made a concerted attack on the merchantman. Several bombs exploded in the water just off her port side and one of these was so close that the blast fractured her fuel lines and disabled her engine. Destroyer *Zulu* took her in tow but this proved a desperately difficult task and progress was painfully slow.

At this point, the convoy at last received some aerial protection in the form of four long-range Beaufighters from Malta. These kept the enemy aircraft away until about 1700 when a shortage of fuel forced them to return to base. *Rowallan Castle* was then attacked almost at once by eleven more Ju 88s and a couple of Italian torpedo-bombers. A furious barrage from the escorting naval vessels thwarted their efforts and darkness finally brought these to an end. It was clear, though, that *Rowallan Castle* would still be outside the range of Malta's Hurricanes by the time dawn brought a renewal of the raids and both she and *Zulu* towing her would then be 'sitting ducks'. Her crew was therefore taken off and, like *Clan Chattan*, she was sunk by destroyers' torpedoes. No supplies at all would now reach Malta.

It was a calamity, bad enough in itself but boding worse for the future. When General Brooke, always very conscious of the value of Malta, heard the news, he noted in his diary: 'These are black days.' Even Admiral Cunningham was daunted. He and his fellow commanders-in-chief in the Middle East, Auchinleck and Air Marshal Sir Arthur Tedder, advised the chiefs of staff that: 'It appears useless to try to pass in a convoy until the air situation in Malta has been restored and the military situation in Cyrenaica improved.' The chiefs of staff retorted that Malta was so important that it must be supplied and 'no consideration of risk to ships need to deter you.' The ships aiding Malta would certainly continue to be at risk and to suffer accordingly. Malta's governor, Lieutenant General Sir William Dobbie, warned the islanders that they must be prepared for increasing hardships. His warnings were entirely justified.

Notes

1. 'Bf' was short for *Bayerische Flugzeugwerke*: Bavarian Aircraft Company. The abbreviation 'Me', though widely used, was not officially correct until 1944.
2. Schulz was also commissioned as an *oberleutnant* (flying officer). He was credited with an eventual total of fifty-one victories, forty-two of them in the desert, before being killed in action on 17 June 1942. The identity of the British pilot who shot him down remains unknown.
3. The Albacore was basically a later version of the famous Swordfish. Like the Swordfish, it was a biplane but it had closed cockpits and a more powerful, if unfortunately less reliable engine.
4. These are described in great detail in *Malta: The Spitfire Year, 1942* by Christopher Shores and Brian Cull with Nicola Malizia, on which the present account of them is largely based. Spitfires first reached Malta on 7 March. It is a measure of the importance with which Malta was viewed that these were the first Spitfires, apart from a few reconnaissance machines, to operate outside the British Isles.
5. *Clan Campbell* was forced to seek shelter in Tobruk, the nearest British-occupied port. Here her injuries were patched up and she returned safely to Alexandria. She was sunk by air-attack on 23 March while making another attempt to run supplies to Malta.

Chapter 4

Channel Dash

At the heart of Britain's difficulties in keeping Malta supplied was a more fundamental problem, one that limited all Britain's plans and blighted all her prospects: a shortage of shipping. She simply did not possess enough suitable freighters, tankers and troopships, or enough warships to support and protect those she did have. In the last three months of 1941, half-a-dozen of the Royal Navy's capital ships had been lost or disabled: *Prince of Wales*, *Repulse*, *Ark Royal*, battleship *Barham* sunk by a U-boat in the eastern Mediterranean, battleships *Queen Elizabeth* and *Valiant* crippled by Italian 'human torpedoes' in Alexandria Harbour. Two fleet carriers, a light carrier and five battleships as well as cruisers and destroyers needed to be sent to oppose the Japanese in the Indian Ocean. Add responsibilities in the Mediterranean, and it is not surprising that Britain's naval strength, even in her home waters, was far from impressive.

The warships in Britain's Home Fleet also had a multitude of duties. By a curious coincidence, the political leaders on both sides had their eyes fixed on Norway. Churchill tells us that he argued for an invasion of Norway throughout most of 1942, though without success. It seems almost as if Hitler had read Churchill's mind, for he was adamant that such an invasion would be attempted and held back both U-boats and surface vessels in order to oppose this. In particular, Germany's giant battleship *Tirpitz* moved to Trondheim in mid-January.

Although *Tirpitz* could be no threat to an invasion of Norway since none was planned, she presented a very real and grave danger to British shipping. It was possible that she might break out into the North Atlantic to prey on British merchantmen there. It was probable that she would fall on the Allies' Arctic convoys carrying vital material to the Russian ports of Murmansk and Archangel. Bad weather in early February allowed the ten ships of Convoy PQ9/10 (they had originally formed two separate convoys but these had later been combined) and the thirteen ships of PQ11 to reach Russia undetected, while two convoys returning from Russia also made their perilous passage with little interference from the enemy. It was accepted, however, that such good fortune might well not continue.

Accordingly Admiral Sir John Tovey, Commander-in-Chief, Home Fleet, was compelled to keep all four of his capital ships – battleship *King George V*, aircraft carrier *Victorious* and two elderly vessels, battleship *Rodney* and battle-cruiser *Renown*, not to mention escorting cruisers and destroyers – in northern waters so as to oppose *Tirpitz* if this proved necessary. 'As long as she was present in Norway,' observes Captain Stephen Roskill in the British Official History of *The War at Sea*, 'her influence was bound to make itself felt in all the waters from Murmansk to the American seaboard, for which the Home Fleet was mainly responsible.'

Nor was it only British warships that were tied down by *Tirpitz*; British aircraft were also affected. Carrier-based torpedo-planes would not be able to use their weapons in the narrow, steep-sided fjord in which the battleship was moored. She was all but out of range of heavy bombers and an attempted raid in late January was totally unsuccessful. Yet she had to be watched and in the prevailing weather conditions, the only reconnaissance aircraft that could do this effectively were Mosquitos, then in very short supply. Moreover, torpedo-bombers had to be kept in the north, ready to attack her if she managed to break out and these also flew wasteful armed reconnaissance patrols in case she did so undetected by the Mosquitos.

If Britain's major warships were thus engaged in guarding against sorties by their German and Japanese equivalents, her smaller warships from destroyers downwards were employed on the arduous task of protecting convoys, not only in the Arctic but, to a much greater extent, in the Atlantic. As it happened, during February 1942 there were few attacks on convoys in the North Atlantic as the U-boats had found easier prey elsewhere. Of course, in February 1942 no theatre of war could expect to escape without at least one unpleasant incident and in the North Atlantic this duly came about on the 22nd. A U-boat 'pack' detected Convoy ON67 en route to Britain and 'in a three-day battle' reports Captain Roskill, they 'sank eight ships, six of which were large tankers, without loss'.

At the time the submarines appeared, Convoy ON67 was escorted by four American destroyers. This was a somewhat ironic circumstance because, when attempting to combat the U-boats in their own home waters, the Americans, as Captain Roskill points out, 'tried every conceivable measure – except convoy and escort.'

In fact the Americans were quite unprepared, mentally and materially, to combat the U-boats at all. On the entry of the United States into the war, Admiral Karl Dönitz, Hitler's commander of the submarine service, at once prepared for an assault on the shipping lanes running past America's east coast. By February, the U-boats were regularly slaughtering merchantmen in general and tankers in particular, virtually without opposition and in many cases aided by having their victims silhouetted against waterfront lights in cities along the coast; proposals to shut these down were met by protests that it would ruin the tourist trade.

In mid-February the submarines extended the area of their depredations into the Caribbean Sea and as far south as the mainland of South America. Again, tankers were their principal targets and, encouraged by a continuing lack of effective retaliation, they became ever more daring. On 16 February, they sank four tankers at or near the valuable oil port of Aruba near Curaçao in the Dutch West Indies, and also shelled shore installations though without inflicting serious damage. On the 18th, the boldest of all the U-boat commanders, *Kapitänleutnant* (Lieutenant Commander) Albrecht Achilles took *U-161* into the harbour of Port of Spain, Trinidad, where he sank two merchantmen at anchor. He followed this up by making a similar penetration of Castries Harbour, Saint Lucia, where *U-161* torpedoed a freighter and a passenger-steamer.

In all, February 1942 saw eighty-five ships, a total of 476,451 tons, sunk by U-boats, the majority of them in the western Atlantic or the Caribbean. This was the greatest number lost so far in any month of the war. There were fewer British vessels sunk than American, but almost all the casualties were Allied vessels – though the Germans did not spare neutrals either – and they would be urgently needed in the future. In addition, they took with them to the bottom supplies that would have helped to sustain the British war effort.

Inevitably, therefore, much British interest was directed onto the events taking place on the far side of the Atlantic. On 10 February Britain, without being asked, suggested sending ten corvettes and twenty-four anti-submarine trawlers, all with experienced crews, to the danger zone; an offer gladly accepted by the Americans. All these circumstances tended to reduce the attention paid to another aspect of the Atlantic battle, one that had now been a continuing problem for several months.

While the U-boat was the most potent threat to Britain's lifelines, it was not the only one: there was the surface raider to consider as well. A year earlier in February 1941, the German battle-cruisers *Scharnhorst* and *Gneisenau* broke out into the North Atlantic. They had been ordered to avoid convoys with a strong escort, but at that time it was customary for westbound convoys to be dispersed and for individual ships to head for different destinations in North America. During February and March, the raiders sank twenty-two unescorted merchantmen, totalling 115,600 tons. They then headed for Brest, which they entered on the morning of 22 March. Bad weather prevented their presence being detected by aerial reconnaissance until the 28th, but thereafter they were kept under constant observation by the RAF's No. 1 Photographic Reconnaissance Unit (PRU), which in the months to come was to fly 729 sorties for this purpose and to lose nine of its aircraft in the process.

That the battle-cruisers might emerge from Brest to renew their depredations in the Atlantic was a threat that could not be ignored and hung over all Britain's plans for conducting the war at sea. On the other hand, their presence in the French port held out the possibility of attacking them there with heavy bombers or torpedo-planes. It would mean diverting RAF Bomber Command from its assault on the cities of Germany and would entail considerable risks, for Brest was known to have strong AA defences and its distance from British bases meant that it would be difficult to provide the bombers with a fighter escort. Yet Churchill demanded that attempts must be made to destroy the 'Ugly Sisters' as the RAF unkindly called them, regardless of losses.

For a week after the Ugly Sisters had first been sighted and despite continuing bad weather, RAF Halifaxes and Stirlings, 200 aircraft in all, did fly a series of missions in an attempt to meet the prime minister's wishes. They made no hits, but on 5 April a bomb fell dangerously near to the dock that contained *Gneisenau* and failed to explode. While a bomb-disposal team set about rendering this harmless, *Gneisenau* was moved into the inner harbour. Later that day, one of 1 PRU's indefatigable reconnaissance Spitfires revealed her new position and in the early hours of 6 April, six Beaufort torpedo-bombers of Coastal Command's 22 Squadron were made ready to attack her.

Once more the airmen had to struggle against the weather as well as the enemy. So bad were the conditions at No. 22's base, St Eval in Cornwall, that only four Beauforts were able to take off. Over Brest, a thick haze covered the target. Just one torpedo-bomber could locate *Gneisenau* and to reach her this would have to pass three heavily-armed flak-ships moored in the outer harbour, cross over a long stone mole surrounding the inner harbour, and face the 270 anti-aircraft guns protecting it.

Despite the appalling odds against him, the Beaufort's pilot, Flying Officer Kenneth Campbell, went in on his own. Bursting past the startled flak-ships at less than mast-height, he hurtled over the mole and released his torpedo. Then the Beaufort, torn apart by a concentrated crossfire, crashed into the harbour. Campbell, who was awarded a posthumous Victoria Cross, and his loyal crew – Sergeants Scott, Mullis and Hillman – had no chance of surviving; they were buried by the Germans in the cemetery at Brest with full military honours.

They did not live to see the success their sacrifice had brought. Their torpedo struck *Gneisenau* beneath the waterline near her stern. Desperate efforts kept her afloat and finally got her into dry dock early the next day, but it was eight months before her repairs were completed and she was soon to suffer further harm. On the night of 10/11 April, a raid by Bomber Command scored four hits and two near misses that caused considerable damage, including putting one of her turrets out of action.

In this same attack, dock facilities were wrecked, with the result that *Scharnhorst*, though not hurt directly, was for a time unable to proceed with her refitting. Consequently, neither of the Ugly Sisters was available for a great pincer movement on the convoy routes planned by the Germans for May 1941. The vessels intended to form the northern arm of the pincers – the giant battleship *Bismarck* and the heavy cruiser *Prinz Eugen* – proceeded on their mission alone but after a brief, brilliant action in the Denmark Strait when she sank the British battle-cruiser *Hood*, *Bismarck* was fatally crippled by a torpedo launched from one of *Ark Royal*'s Swordfish and finished off by overwhelming odds. *Prinz Eugen* had parted company from the battleship earlier and reached Brest safely on 1 June, her arrival being confirmed three days later by a 'recce' Spitfire.

The RAF pilots considered that *Prinz Eugen* was 'a beautiful ship' and never ranked her as a third Ugly Sister. This, though, did not save her from the raids that continued at regular intervals and on the night of 1/2 July a bomb hit her foredeck, killing fifty-one of her crew and putting her out of action. The lucky *Scharnhorst* was still untouched and later in the month completed her refit. On the 22nd a reconnaissance Spitfire caused consternation when it reported that *Scharnhorst* had left Brest, but on the following day another Spitfire sighted her at La Pallice near La Rochelle where she intended to carry out her sea trials without interference from the air. Two heavy, if ineffective raids that night showed that these hopes were illusory and on the 24th, a daylight attack by Halifaxes cost the RAF five aircraft but scored five hits on the battle-cruiser. Though two of the bombs failed to explode, the others caused such damage that *Scharnhorst* was forced to return to Brest with 3,000 tons of water flooding her. She reached Brest safely, but many weeks would pass before her repairs were completed.

Frequent light raids, varied by occasional heavy ones, continued for the rest of the year. On the night of 3/4 September, fifty-six bombers attacked Brest and 120 more did the same ten days later.

Neither raid did any damage, nor did a further assault by 101 aircraft on the night of 17/18 December. This was followed on the afternoon of the 18th by a forty-one-strong attack that cost the RAF six heavy bombers but hit the lock gates of the dock containing *Scharnhorst*, thereby preventing her from moving into the harbour for a month. In the same raid, *Gneisenau* received minor damage and she was again slightly damaged on 6 January 1942.

By February 1942, however, Ultra interceptions warned that *Scharnhorst*, *Gneisenau* and *Prinz Eugen* were all ready to go to sea and likely to do so in the near future. Photographic reconnaissance confirmed that the three of them were now out of dry dock and also reported the arrival in Brest of minesweepers, E-boats (as German motor-torpedo-boats were called), and, most ominously, six big destroyers, clearly intended to act as escorts for the larger warships when they sailed. It was possible that they would renew their assault on the Atlantic convoys and it was with this in mind that Force H, as we saw earlier, was transferred from Gibraltar to the Clyde to provide protection for a troop convoy. Ironically, by the time this sailed, the Brest warships were no longer a threat to it.

This was due to Hitler deciding that it would be better to station the Brest Group in Norway where it could join *Tirpitz* in threatening the Arctic convoys and guarding against that invasion which Churchill always wanted and the Führer feared would deprive him of Norwegian iron ore and of his chance to disrupt the supply route to Russia. His decision was strongly opposed by the members of his Naval War Staff headed by Grand Admiral Erich Raeder. They argued that the presence of major German warships in Brest presented a threat to the Atlantic convoys, increased British anxieties and tied down British naval forces, and these advantages would be lost if *Scharnhorst*, *Gneisenau* and *Prinz Eugen* were withdrawn from the French port.

Raeder therefore considered Hitler's determination to do just that was a strategic mistake. It is easy to sympathize with him, particularly since a British invasion of Norway was never planned and most later commentators have echoed his views and indulged in heavy sarcasm at the expense of Hitler's 'intuition'. Thereby, though, they probably do Hitler an injustice: it would appear that in this instance at least, he had thought very carefully before deciding on the best course of action.

One factor influencing Hitler was the loss of the *Bismarck*. This had led him to query the effectiveness of employing his surface warships on raids into the Atlantic and his doubts had been shared by Admiral Dönitz. Hitler had considered the strategic advantages of having a naval force at Brest, but in a conference in Berlin on 12 January 1942 he expressed a belief that 'enemy sea forces' were held down by the ships in Brest 'to no greater extent than if the ships were stationed in Norway'. On the other hand, he acknowledged the 'welcome effect' of the Brest Group in 'tying up enemy air forces and diverting them from making attacks upon the German homeland.'

In conclusion, Hitler agreed that if he could see any chance that his warships in Brest 'might remain undamaged for four or five months' then he might be inclined to leave them where they were, but he could not accept that this was likely to happen. Even his naval advisers were compelled to concede that the warships had all been hit in the past and *Reichsmarschall* Hermann Göring had bluntly told him that the Luftwaffe could not undertake to prevent further injuries in the future. Raeder would later complain that Göring could have provided adequate aerial protection had he wished but Göring, who had to accept commitments in Russia and North Africa and the need to guard the cities of Germany from Bomber Command, had every reason for his assertion.

The British, Hitler pointed out, would clearly not need to guard against sorties by the Brest warships if these were sunk or crippled and the diversion of the RAF would 'last exactly as long as the enemy considers himself compelled to attack because the ships are undamaged.' Since it seemed that the strategic advantages of keeping his vessels in Brest were likely to be lost in the near future anyhow, Hitler felt it would be only sensible to get them away while they were still intact and could be of use to him elsewhere. The naval officers reluctantly bowed to the Führer's will, only to be horrified by hearing how he proposed to bring about the Brest Group's retirement.

Hitler's naval advisers had always considered that if the warships were to leave Brest, whether for Germany or Norway, they should break out into the Atlantic and pass north of the British Isles. 'An unobserved and safe escape' through the English Channel, declared Admiral Raeder, would be 'impossible'. Hitler again thought otherwise. He believed that the route favoured by the Naval War Staff would be at risk from attack by the British Home Fleet which he knew was stationed in the north. At the conference of 12 January, he therefore flatly announced that *Scharnhorst, Gneisenau* and *Prinz Eugen* would make for Germany – and thence of course for Norway – by way of the Channel and planning for this was to be started at once.

That the 'Channel Dash', as it would become known, was a daring gamble was obvious to all and Hitler laid down some important requirements for success. Surprise he rightly regarded as essential. Accordingly, strict security precautions were imposed, knowledge of the plan was limited to a few crucial officers and all movements by the major warships were kept to a minimum so that Britain's aerial scouts would not suspect that any action was about to happen.

The demands of surprise also dictated Hitler's choice for the timing of the operation. It would not be possible for his ships to complete their journey through the Channel in a single day, so they would have either to make the first part in darkness and be prepared for a passage of the Straits of Dover in daylight, or cross the greater part of the Channel by day and enjoy the cover of night when they entered the Straits of Dover. Hitler unhesitatingly chose the first alternative. If his warships left Brest by day, there was every prospect that they would be sighted early on and the British given plenty of time to prepare attacks on them. If they left in darkness, they might hope to escape detection until the next morning when the majority of their journey would lie behind them. Admittedly, they were likely to face attacks from sea and air in the narrowest part of the Channel, but these would have to be hurriedly improvised, the Germans would be able to see them coming and any air-raids could be opposed by covering fighters, of which Hitler demanded that the maximum possible be provided.

Having laid down his fundamental requirements, Hitler left it to trusted subordinates to work out the details of the plan. The naval aspect became the responsibility of Vice Admiral Otto Ciliax, a harsh, unpopular but very able officer who did not at first like the idea of a Channel Dash, but after due consideration concluded that it had a good chance of success. He decided that the operation should commence at 1930 on 11 February, a dark night four days after the new moon and one when a spring tide would be moving up the Channel to increase the speed of his vessels' progress.

Ciliax would fly his flag in *Scharnhorst* which would lead out the three major warships. They would be protected by the six destroyers that had joined them in Brest and these would be reinforced at intervals by E-boats, totalling thirty-four eventually. Minesweepers would be sent ahead to clear a safe passage and arrangements made to jam British radar stations to reduce the chance of early detection.

To co-ordinate the required air cover, Hitler chose the German ace Adolf Galland, recently promoted to General of Fighters, and personally instructed him on the importance of his task. Galland then went aboard *Scharnhorst* to discuss the operation with Ciliax. To ensure effective liaison, he installed on *Scharnhorst* a fighter control team under Colonel Max Ibel and on both the other major warships a controller and a radio operator. Aircraft were sent to France from Germany and Norway and with these reinforcements Galland was able to provide a sequence of standing patrols, each of sixteen fighters, mainly new Messerschmitt Bf 109Fs and Focke-Wulf Fw 190s, over the Brest Group for the whole of its daylight passage. Moreover, arrangements were made whereby in the event of an attack, these standing patrols could be joined by Luftwaffe units stationed all along the coasts of France and Holland.

None of these precautions consoled Admiral Raeder and those who shared his opinion that the Channel Dash would result in the destruction of at least one, probably all, of his precious ships. At the 12 January conference, however, all opposition was imperiously overruled by Hitler:

'The Brest Group,' snapped the dictator, 'is like a patient suffering from cancer who is doomed unless he submits to an operation. An operation, on the other hand, even though it might have to be a drastic one, affords at least some hope that

the patient's life might be saved. The passage of the ships
through the Channel will be such an operation and has
therefore to be attempted.'

Having reduced his opponents to depressed silence, Hitler did offer
them one crumb of comfort. 'You may count on this,' he promised.
'From my previous experience I do not believe the British capable of
the conception and execution of lightning decisions such as will be
required for the transfer of their air and sea forces to meet the
boldness of our operation.' It is humiliating to observe that his
judgement would prove absolutely correct.

What makes this episode particularly depressing is the fact that
the Germans' use of the Channel did not in itself help them to
achieve surprise. As far back as April 1941, the British had
considered it possible that the Ugly Sisters might use this escape
route and steps were taken to prepare countermeasures, collectively
known as Operation FULLER. As the months passed and
Intelligence from Ultra and photographic reconnaissance continued
to come in, suspicions hardened and on 2 February 1942, the
Admiralty issued a formal Appreciation. This predicted that the
Brest warships were unlikely to attempt a raid into the Atlantic
because they could not be fully efficient after their long inactivity;
that they would almost certainly attempt to escape through the
Channel; and that this would take place in the very near future.

On 3 February, both the Admiralty and the Air Ministry issued
the signal: 'Executive FULLER'. This brought the naval and air
forces detailed to be ready to oppose a Channel Dash to immediate
readiness. At the same time, arrangements were made to ensure that
the enemy's movements were detected as early as possible. HM
Submarine *Sealion* was ordered to take station off Brest; the regular
searches that were carried out by Coastal Command's radar-
equipped Hudsons over the western parts of the Channel by day and
by night were increased; and Fighter Command sent out pairs of
Spitfires every two hours of daylight on reconnaissance missions
called 'Jim Crows' over the Channel's eastern areas.

Unfortunately, the plans made for FULLER contained several
serious flaws. One was the refusal of the First Sea Lord, Admiral Sir

Dudley Pound, to allow any of his capital ships to be brought south as part of the defending forces, fearing that if they were, they would 'be exposed to enemy air attack, torpedo-boat attack, and risk being damaged by our own or enemy minefields'. Moreover, in February 1942, as already mentioned, the attention of the Home Fleet was firmly directed towards the *Tirpitz* at Trondheim. With the Royal Navy's other commitments, all that could be spared for Vice Admiral Sir Bertram Ramsay, who from his Headquarters at Dover was responsible for the naval side of FULLER, were six destroyers and a handful of motor-torpedo-boats.

This in effect transferred the role of stopping a Channel Dash to the Royal Air Force, which in theory made considerable numbers of aircraft available for FULLER. Air Marshal Sir Richard Peirse, head of Bomber Command, originally set aside 300 of his warplanes, of which perhaps 240 were serviceable at any one time, as a reserve for use in FULLER; these already had their bombs on board and their crews warned to be ready for action at two hours' notice. Fighter Command was also instructed to be prepared to provide protection for any bombers ordered off against the Brest Group. As time passed, however, Peirse understandably became concerned at having so much of his strength thus in practice lying idle, unable to carry out any training, let alone what Bomber Command considered its proper task, the attacks on German cities.[1] Therefore on 10 February, on his own responsibility and unhappily without warning the Admiralty of his decision, Peirse reduced the number of bombers ready for FULLER to 100 and put the crews of these on four hours' notice.

In any event, the crews of Peirse's heavy bombers were not properly trained for attacks on warships at sea. This was appreciated and as a result, the planners of FULLER placed most of their confidence in torpedo-planes, particularly the Beauforts of Coastal Command. The trouble was that the casualties suffered by the Royal Navy in the Mediterranean had led to Churchill sending the majority of the available torpedo-planes to assist in the defence of Egypt.

This meant that there were only three Beaufort squadrons left in Britain and one of them, No. 42, was based at Leuchars in Scotland, ready to engage the *Tirpitz* should she sortie from Trondheim; its fourteen aircraft were ordered south on 8 February, but the move was delayed for several days by heavy snow and dreadful weather conditions generally. Seven Beauforts of 217 Squadron were at Thorney Island near Portsmouth, while the squadron's other three machines were at St Eval in Cornwall together with twelve Beauforts of 86 Squadron.

Finally, at Manston in Kent were the six Swordfish torpedo-bombers of the Fleet Air Arm's 825 Squadron. This had yet to complete its training and many of its personnel were inexperienced, but Lieutenant Commander Eugene Esmonde, an Irishman who had previously led a strike on *Bismarck* from aircraft carrier *Victorious* – an exploit that had earned him a DSO – had volunteered to add his men to the strength of the FULLER forces. The slow, vulnerable Swordfish were hardly suitable for operations where large numbers of enemy fighters were likely to be encountered, but Esmonde had been informed that 825 Squadron would only be attacking under cover of darkness.

This information illustrates another crucial flaw in the planning of FULLER. Ramsay, Peirse, Air Chief Marshal Sir Philip Joubert, head of Coastal Command, and Air Vice-Marshal Trafford Leigh-Mallory who controlled No. 11 Group of Fighter Command, the aircraft of which were responsible for the Jim Crow reconnaissance flights and would provide the escort for any bomber missions, were all convinced that the German warships would make the first part of their move in daylight, timing their advance so as to reach the Straits of Dover after nightfall, the complete opposite of what the enemy really intended.

In view of the valid and cogent reasons that had led to Hitler's decision, it seems surprising that none of the British authorities came to the same conclusion and frankly incredible that they did not at least plan an alternative scenario in case the conclusion that they did come to turned out to be wrong. This error assisted the Germans in achieving surprise and ensured that operations against them would be hasty, improvised and confused. They would also lack co-ordination, mainly as a result of very tight security, surely unnecessary in this case, that resulted in the FULLER plans being known to only a few senior officers and their staffs and not to those who would have to carry them out.

At 1615 on 11 February 1942, a Spitfire flown by Squadron Leader Ball made what would be the last sighting by No. 1 PRU of the major German warships at Brest. Its photographs showed all three of them in the harbour, protected by torpedo booms. This did not suggest a departure in the near future, still less that Vice Admiral Ciliax in fact proposed to put to sea at 1930 that evening. Just as he was on the point of doing so, however, seventeen Wellington bombers arrived to make yet another attack on the Brest Group. The raid scored no hits on any of the German warships and one bomber was brought down by AA fire, but it did result in Ciliax not leaving harbour until 2115, a delay that proved extremely beneficial to the Germans.

As mentioned earlier, HM Submarine *Sealion* had been sent to patrol off Brest. She had taken to moving deep into Iroise Bay, at the head of which Brest stands, every morning and retiring at dusk in order to recharge her batteries. Since, as we have seen, none of the British authorities believed that the Germans would leave Brest after dark, this appeared to be an entirely suitable course of action. Ironically, *Sealion* was still on guard at 1930 when Ciliax had planned to set out, but she withdrew about an hour later and so failed to sight his actual departure a further three-quarters of an hour after that.

There were still three chances of the Channel Dash being detected on the night of 11/12 February, in the form of three patrol lines, each flown by a succession of Hudsons from Coastal Command. The darkness was intense – it was said that the crews of the Hudsons could hardly make out the wing-tips of their own aircraft – and although they were of course fitted with radar sets capable in theory of detecting a ship at a range of some 30 miles, these were generally regarded as unreliable and not infrequently broke down altogether.

A whole succession of misfortunes now occurred. The radar of the first Hudson to fly the most westerly of the patrol lines failed and its crew had to return to base. They resumed their watch in another aircraft until just before midnight when their term of duty ended. As ill luck would have it, the German fleet never quite came within radar range of this aircraft. It did come briefly within range of the next Hudson to fly this patrol line, but no revealing 'blip' appeared on the screen and it would seem that this set had also had its problems but that these had remained undetected.

There is no argument that the radar of the Hudson on the second patrol line failed altogether and it had to return to its base. Because of a shortage of aircraft, it could not be replaced immediately and so when the Brest Group crossed this patrol line it was not in fact being patrolled. Neither was the third and last patrol line, because the Hudson that ought to have sighted the escaping warships had been recalled early in view of a forecast of dawn fog over its airfield. It may be added that not one of these misfortunes was reported to Vice Admiral Ramsay at Dover, probably because they were not considered significant: after all, the British had concluded that the enemy would never attempt the first part of the Channel Dash after dark.

Britain's radar stations on shore did not detect the German vessels either. The enemy had for some weeks been jamming reception by these, usually in short bursts that suggested natural atmospherics and increasing their interference steadily but slowly so as not to excite suspicion. By 12 February, the jamming had become accepted as routine and such 'blips' as did appear were interpreted at first as coastal shipping or aircraft on air-sea rescue exercises; the majority of those who observed them felt no alarm because the strict security that had been imposed meant that few people even knew about Operation FULLER.

As the morning wore on, however, some of those who did know began to have doubts, in particular Wing Commander Jarvis, Senior Controller of the Radar Filter Room at Fighter Command Headquarters, Bentley Priory; Squadron Leader Igoe, the Controller at Biggin Hill aerodrome; and Flight Lieutenant Kidd, the station commander at Swingate airfield, Dover. Kidd telephoned Wing Commander Constable-Roberts, Ramsay's air liaison officer, who in turn rang the headquarters of Fighter Command's No. 11 Group. Jarvis and Igoe contacted No. 11 Group direct. None of them received any satisfaction. Leigh-Mallory was away reviewing a parade of Belgian airmen, and his staff officers showed no concern over or indeed interest in the reports.

In an attempt to clarify the situation one way or the other, Igoe, on his own initiative, contacted Squadron Leader Robert Oxspring, CO of 91 (Spitfire) Squadron based at Hawkinge and requested that he investigate the 'blips' revealed on the radar screens; however, he did not mention Operation FULLER because of the security clampdown. Oxspring and Sergeant Beaumont took off at 1020, believing they were merely engaged on a standard reconnaissance flight. They sighted a group of Messerschmitt Bf 109Fs but evaded these by taking cover in low clouds; then, through pouring rain, they sighted the Brest Group. At this time, there was a strict order in force at No. 11 Group forbidding any pilot to break radio silence, but Oxspring felt that this situation called on him to make an exception to the rule. He therefore broadcast the sighting report: 'Three large German ships, probably battle-cruisers'.

Still no countermeasures were put in hand. It appears that Oxspring's message was never received or just possibly it was received but was disbelieved and so disregarded; at any rate no action was taken. The Spitfires returned to Hawkinge at 1050 and after talking to Igoe, Oxspring made yet another telephone call to No. 11 Group. This had no effect either.

Luckily, another pair of Spitfire pilots sighted the Brest Group shortly after Oxspring. Group Captain Victor Beamish as Leigh-Mallory's Senior Air Staff Officer was not really supposed to be making flights across the Channel but he was a fighting Ulsterman who, when station commander at North Weald during the Battle of Britain, had taken off with the squadrons based there at every opportunity. He was now the station commander at Kenley and was constantly to be found accompanying the Kenley Wing. By way of variety, he would also often set out with one companion – on 12 February this was another Battle of Britain veteran, Wing Commander Richard Finlay Boyd – 'with the idea of picking up a stray Hun.'[2]

Near the French coast, Beamish and Boyd sighted a pair of 109s and were pursuing these when they found themselves racing over the German fleet. Risking its anti-aircraft fire, they flew across it at low level, then climbed into cloud to avoid the fighter escort and made for base at top speed. As an important staff officer, Beamish did know all about Operation FULLER and he appreciated immediately that he had encountered the warships from Brest. Had he radioed his sighting – the one word 'FULLER' would have been enough – he might have saved precious time, but since it was he who had signed the order forbidding pilots to break radio silence, he felt that it would be wrong if he, of all people, disregarded it.

Beamish and Boyd landed at 1110 and the former joined the queue of those telephoning No. 11 Group. As the highest-ranking officer in the queue, he did manage to get through to Leigh-Mallory who at first was not pleased to have been disturbed. Beamish managed to pacify him and then convince him of the importance of the sighting. At about 1135, Leigh-Mallory at last sent out the necessary warning to all British authorities concerned with the execution of Operation FULLER. At 1215, Vice Admiral Ciliax had notice of the first attempts to check his progress when shore batteries opened fire on his force, though none of their shells came anywhere near it. *Scharnhorst*, *Gneisenau* and *Prinz Eugen* had by then already passed through the Straits of Dover. Their passage, according to Ciliax, 'was no more difficult than an exercise in home waters.'

Thereafter the Brest Group would experience plenty of opposition, but this was piecemeal and unco-ordinated and could hardly hope to inflict much damage. The first attempt was made by five motor-torpedo-boats from Dover, led by Lieutenant Commander Nigel Pumphrey. They sighted the enemy at 1223. Harried by fire from E-boats and destroyers and strafed by German fighters, all of them managed to launch two torpedoes at the major German warships, though at long range and without success, before retiring under a smokescreen laid by two motor-gunboats from Dover that arrived at just the right moment. They then decided not to return to harbour immediately as it seemed likely that they might be able to help survivors from another attack that they had just seen being delivered.

Lieutenant Commander Esmonde's 825 Squadron had been given more notice than most units. After failing to get a satisfactory response from No. 11 Group, Wing Commander Constable-Roberts had attempted to arouse the interest of Coastal Command, again without success. He had then telephoned Esmonde, told him of his suspicions and suggested that the Swordfish be loaded with their torpedoes. When formal confirmation of his fears was received, Constable-Roberts at 1140 again rang Manston airfield to pass on the news to Esmonde and to the station commander Wing Commander Thomas Gleave.[3] Group Captain Beamish, on his own initiative, also telephoned Gleave and told him: 'FULLER – get cracking, Tom, lad.'

Esmonde was now placed in a terrible dilemma. His squadron had volunteered for and trained for an attack under the protection of darkness. It would have been perfectly proper for him to refuse to lead his men in a daylight raid with unsuitable aircraft against a heavily-defended target. Vice Admiral Ramsay was so concerned about the appalling risks involved that, on his instructions, Constable-Roberts again phoned Esmonde to ask how he felt about 'going in'. It was made clear that this would be entirely Esmonde's own decision.

Yet Esmonde was a man with an extremely high sense of duty and honour, strengthened by an unshakeable conviction in the rightness of the Allied cause. Also just prior to hearing from Constable-Roberts, he had been informed that three squadrons of Spitfires would escort the Swordfish and two other Spitfire squadrons would precede them and help to prepare the way for their attacks by strafing the enemy's E-boats and destroyers. This seemed to promise that the risks involved in 825's mission, while still very great, might not prove impossibly high. He declared that his squadron would take off at 1225 and if the Spitfires had not arrived by then, he would rendezvous with them in the air.

Even with the promised fighter support, Esmonde was agonizingly aware of the magnitude of the ordeal he was asking his inexperienced crewmen to undertake. Gleave met him as he walked towards his Swordfish and was shocked to see that Esmonde's eyes were 'dulled' and his face 'grey almost haggard'. To Gleave it seemed 'the face of a man already dead'. As the six old biplanes lumbered into the air, Gleave stood beside the runway and saluted each as it passed him.

In fact, the promised fighter support did not materialize. Four of the Spitfire squadrons, hastily and inadequately briefed, were unable to reach Manston in time, though they subsequently engaged German fighters in combat. Just ten Spitfires from 72 Squadron under Squadron Leader Brian Kingcombe appeared at 1228 and their only instructions had been to escort the Swordfish, no mention being made of the real reason for the sortie or the presence of German capital ships. Esmonde, however, knowing the slow speed of his torpedo-laden Swordfish, decided that he could delay no longer; perhaps he also hoped that the other fighters would arrive before he made his attack. With their meagre escort, the six Swordfish struggled through rain and low cloud towards their mighty enemy.

Tragedy was inevitable. Before the Swordfish had even sighted the major German warships, they were attacked by Messerschmitt Bf 109s: 72 Squadron's Spitfires drove these off, but not before they had damaged most of the Swordfish and caused their formation to split up. Already 825 Squadron had been proceeding in two flights of three aircraft each and now the second flight led by Lieutenant John Thompson fell half-a-mile behind Esmonde's flight. Esmonde's two wingmen, Sub-Lieutenants Brian Rose and Charles Kingsmill, also began to lag behind their leader.

At 1250 the German fleet came into view and above it a strong force of 109s and Focke-Wulf Fw 190s. These promptly rushed to engage the Swordfish as they flew towards their targets through a smokescreen laid by E-boats. Esmonde's machine was set on fire near the tail. Kingcombe's men were again trying to hold off the German fighters and Flight Lieutenant Michael Crombie watched in amazement as Esmonde's telegraphist/air gunner, Leading Airman Clinton, climbed out of his cockpit, crawled down the fuselage, beat out the flames and then made his way back to man his gun. Esmonde was now heading straight for *Prinz Eugen* and the cruiser's 8-inch guns joined in the barrage directed at the Swordfish, one shell striking it and ripping off most of the biplane's lower port wing. Still Esmonde maintained his course.

Then the 109s attacked again. *Leutnant* Egon Mayer poured fire into Esmonde's Swordfish, killing Clinton and the observer Lieutenant Williams and mortally wounding Esmonde; when his body was washed ashore later, there was a line of bullet-holes down his back from neck to waist. As his last action, Esmonde released his torpedo and then the Swordfish crashed into the sea. The torpedo ran on towards *Prinz Eugen* but she evaded it.

Mayer and his wingman *Feldwebel* (Sergeant) Stratmann also attacked the Swordfish of Rose and Kingsmill.[4] Rose was badly wounded and his gunner Leading Airman Johnson, one of 825 Squadron's few experienced personnel who had been awarded a Distinguished Service Medal at the time of the *Bismarck* operation, was killed instantly. Rose's observer, Sub-Lieutenant Edgar Lee, stood upright in his cockpit, looking back towards the attacking German fighters, shouting warnings to take evasive action when he estimated these would open fire. Rose, fighting to remain conscious, launched his torpedo at *Prinz Eugen*, passed right over the cruiser and subsequently ditched beyond the E-boats on the enemy's starboard flank.

Sub-Lieutenant Kingsmill's Swordfish was the last of the first flight to attack *Prinz Eugen*. By that time the pilot and his observer Sub-Lieutenant Samples had both been wounded; Leading Airman Bunce, Kingsmill's gunner, was miraculously unhurt, though cannon shells had torn out the bottom part of the fuselage just below his cockpit. After dropping his torpedo, Kingsmill turned away over the rear of the German warships, in the process coming under further flak that started a fire. He too managed to ditch and he and his crew were rescued by one of the British motor-torpedo-boats, as later were Rose and Lee. Neither of the torpedoes launched by Rose and Kingsmill found its mark.

The three Swordfish in the second flight had no chance of launching torpedoes. They flew through the first barrage sent up by the E-boats on the Germans' port flank, only to be attacked head-on by a group of Focke-Wulf Fw 190s. The leader of these, *Leutnant* Johannes Naumann, personally shot down Thompson's Swordfish and the aircraft flown by Sub-Lieutenants Wood and Bligh quickly followed it into the sea. There were no survivors.[5]

In the opinion of Vice Admiral Ramsay, the sortie of the six Swordfish was 'one of the finest exhibitions of self-sacrifice and devotion to duty that the war has yet witnessed' and he deplored the failure to provide them with an adequate fighter escort. Vice Admiral Ciliax agreed that their bravery 'surpasses any other action by either side that day'. On the recommendation of Wing Commander Gleave, Esmonde, an officer not under Gleave's command and from a different service, was awarded a posthumous Victoria Cross. Rose, Lee, Kingsmill and Samples each received a Distinguished Service Order – a considerable distinction for junior officers – and Bunce a rare Conspicuous Gallantry Medal. All the remaining members of 825 Squadron were Mentioned in Despatches, the only decoration apart from the VC that could be given to a serviceman who had died in action.

Prinz Eugen and her Ugly Sisters suffered no more air attacks for some time, although small sections of cannon-armed Hurricane fighters and 'Hurribombers' (Hurricanes armed with bombs) made several strikes on the smaller escort vessels. A particularly daring one took place at 1430, when six Hurricanes from No. 1 Squadron led by Flight Lieutenant Raymond attacked three of the German destroyers, two fighters for each. Flying through a violent AA barrage, the Hurricanes came in at 50 feet, their cannon shells striking the warships' decks and superstructures and causing some damage and casualties. Only four Hurricanes returned to base.

Just one minute after the Hurricanes attacked, the immunity of the German capital ships finally ended. An explosion shook the *Scharnhorst* and she slowed to a halt, the victim of a British mine. Vice Admiral Ciliax and his staff transferred to destroyer *Z-29* which set off after the main force, leaving the battle-cruiser behind. Despite damage to her propeller shafts, however, her injuries did not prove serious and she was soon able to get under way again and work up to a speed of 25 knots. Her misfortune at least meant that she was not at risk when the next British attack commenced.

This was delivered by a force of destroyers from Harwich under the command of Captain Pizey. All of them were over twenty years old and intended for use only as escorts to east coast convoys, not for assaults on major German warships. Moreover, their sortie was not exempt from the confusion that seemed to affect all British activities on 12 February. Ten Whirlwind twin-engined long-range fighters were sent out to provide protection from air attacks but they failed to find the destroyers; instead they met enemy warplanes and four of them were shot down. As a further misfortune, destroyer *Walpole* suffered problems with her engines and had to return to port, leaving just five: *Campbell, Vivacious, Worcester, Mackay* and *Whitshed.*

At 1543, the destroyers sighted what they believed were *Scharnhorst* and *Gneisenau* but in reality were *Gneisenau* and *Prinz Eugen.* Scattering the E-boats nearest to them, all five moved in to engage the battle-cruiser, firing their guns and ignoring the heavy shells hurled at them by both the major German warships. The weather was rapidly worsening with mist and rain dramatically reducing visibility and it was probably this that allowed four of the destroyers to launch their torpedoes at *Gneisenau* and retire undamaged.

The fifth destroyer, the *Worcester*, was less fortunate. Lieutenant Commander Coates, misled by a faulty range-finder, came in closest to *Gneisenau* before firing his torpedoes and suffered for it: 11-inch shells from the battle-cruiser found their mark in *Worcester*'s boiler rooms, bringing her to a halt broadside-on to *Prinz Eugen.* The cruiser's gunners took full advantage of this easy target and four salvoes of 8-inch shells struck *Worcester*, wrecking her guns, bridge and wireless room, tearing huge holes in her side and starting fires. Miraculously only four men died and nineteen more were wounded but to observers on both sides it seemed that *Worcester* was doomed.

This was also the opinion of Lieutenant Commander Coates, who gave the order: 'Prepare to abandon ship.' Amid the noise of gunfire, flames and hissing steam, many of the crew did not hear their skipper's first two words and the wounded were placed on rafts and lowered into the water while many of the unwounded also went over the side, relying on their life-jackets. Yet when *Campbell* and *Vivacious* came alongside, they found *Worcester* not only still afloat but starting to master her fires. Shortly afterwards, she was able to raise steam and could move again, if only slowly. *Campbell* and *Vivacious* rescued the men on rafts or in the water and all four undamaged vessels clustered round *Worcester* to escort her back to port. She entered Harwich under her own power the next morning.

It had been another valiant attack with inadequate strength against impossible odds. It had also been another gallant failure, for none of the destroyers' torpedoes had scored a hit. It had been another example of confusion and lack of co-ordination, for when *Campbell* and *Vivacious* were preparing to assist *Worcester* they had come under a determined but happily ineffectual attack from three Beaufort torpedo-bombers. The pilots were not to blame: quite apart from the dreadful weather, the Admiralty had not notified Bomber or Coastal Command that there would be British warships in the combat zone.

At least this episode provided confirmation, if in an unpleasant form, that Coastal Command was now joining in the assaults on the German warships. So indeed was Bomber Command. As we saw earlier, Bomber Command had set aside 100 aircraft for Operation FULLER and these already had their bombs aboard them. The trouble was that they were semi-armour-piercing bombs that could only be effective if dropped from at least 7,000 feet, and in the prevailing weather conditions there was no way in which the aircraft could sight their target from such a height. It was decided therefore to change them for general-purpose bombs that could be dropped from a much lower level; these could not cause serious injuries but might damage superstructure, inflict casualties and distract attention from Coastal Command's torpedo-planes. At the same time, efforts were hastily made to prepare as many other bombers not on stand-by as possible so that they too could take part in the attacks.

Eventually three waves of bombers totalling 242 machines, mainly Wellingtons and Hampdens, were sent out during the afternoon and early evening, but bad weather and bad communications meant that there was no liaison with the torpedo-planes and very little between the aircraft in each wave which reached the target area in small groups or as individuals. Only thirty-nine of them were able to locate enemy warships and attacks were made at wide intervals from about 1500 to 1815, by which time darkness was closing in. Fifteen bombers were lost and one more crashed on landing. No hits were scored and it would probably have caused little harm if any had been.

More confidence was vested in Coastal Command's three squadrons of Beaufort torpedo-planes, but again bad weather and bad communications ensured that any realistic hopes were quickly dashed. Of those Beauforts nearest to the scene of action – 217

Squadron's seven aircraft at Thorney Island near Portsmouth – three were unserviceable or loaded with bombs. The four with torpedoes set off to Manston where they were supposed to rendezvous with an escort of Spitfires. The only information about their target that their pilots had been given was that it was 'an enemy convoy'.

On arriving at Manston at about 1350, the Beauforts could find no trace of any Spitfires; these had in fact set off for the target area, hoping to meet their charges on the way. After orbiting Manston for some time waiting for their escorts, two of the Beauforts decided to make for the combat zone without them. They failed to find the enemy convoy, returned to Manston and later set out again and attacked one of the battle-cruisers – probably *Gneisenau* – independently and unsuccessfully.

Meanwhile the remaining pair of Beauforts, not having observed the departure of their fellows, landed at Manston where, for the first time, they learned the true nature of their mission. They took off once more, still with no fighter cover, and attacked *Prinz Eugen* but without scoring a hit. The three aircraft left behind at Thorney Island, now serviced and armed with torpedoes, subsequently arrived at Manston and duly attacked the enemy fleet as well, all of them being damaged and one crash-landing on its return. Again, no hits were made.

The next Beaufort squadron to see action was No. 42. It will be remembered that this unit had been ordered south from its base at Leuchars but the move had been delayed. It finally landed at Coltishall near Norwich at 1145, but this was a fighter base and had no facilities for servicing torpedo-bombers. Five of No. 42's machines were either declared unfit to fly or had no weapons: these were supposed to have been brought by road but the icy conditions had prevented their being delivered in time. The nine remaining Beauforts took off for Manston where they had been told they would meet with a fighter escort and also a force of Hudsons that would guide them to the target and assist them by making a diversionary bombing attack. Once more, all they had been advised about the target was that this was 'an enemy convoy' and was in the North Sea.

The disorganization that had so far marked the British

countermeasures now descended into pure farce. There were no fighters at Manston with orders to protect 42 Squadron. There were eleven Hudsons from 407 Squadron Royal Canadian Air Force circling the aerodrome when the Beauforts reached it at about 1450, but these had been instructed not that they were to lead the Beauforts to the battle area but that the Beauforts would lead them. For over half-an-hour, Beauforts and Hudsons orbited Manston, each squadron waiting for the other to set off against the enemy.

Mercifully, 42 Squadron's CO, Squadron Leader Cliff, finally decided that, regardless of orders, this situation could not be allowed to continue. He had been told the approximate position of the so-called enemy convoy before leaving Coltishall, so he now led his men towards this. Six of the Hudsons followed him but the rest remained above Manston, apparently waiting for the promised fighters, and when these still did not appear, they returned to their base.

Now the bad weather again served to hamper, though it also served to protect the British efforts. The Hudsons lost contact with the torpedo-planes and eventually bombed the German destroyer and E-boat screen, but without effect and losing two of their number to AA fire. Three of the Beauforts also became separated from their squadron but Cliff led the other six at very low level against a German warship, probably *Gneisenau*. No hits were made. The three aircraft that had lost touch also engaged vessels dimly sighted through rain and cloud. They reported that one of these was 'listing badly and with smoke pouring from the bow.' This was correct and the vessel in question was the *Worcester*: these were the Beauforts that attacked *Campbell* and *Vivacious*. Luckily, they made no hits either.

There remained only the Beauforts at St Eval. The three from 217 Squadron had been ordered out on patrol over the Bay of Biscay, but 86 Squadron flew its twelve machines to Thorney Island where their torpedoes were fitted. After numerous confused and contradictory instructions they were eventually sent on to Manston, which they reached at about 1700. Although there was – one is tempted to say 'of course' – no sign of a promised fighter escort, the Beauforts were notified of the location of what was still being described as an enemy convoy and took off to search for this. In worsening weather and growing darkness they failed to find it but they did sight four German minesweepers. These put up a heavy barrage of AA fire and two of the Beauforts failed to return to base.

This marked the end of Coastal Command's attempts to attack the Brest Group. Two night-flying Beaufighters that were also sent out by Coastal Command sighted some of the German warships at about 1800, but their orders were only to shadow the enemy, not assault him. The efforts of Bomber Command have already been related. In addition, the RAF had employed Spitfires, Hurricanes and Whirlwinds, 341 fighters in all if one may include eighteen Hurribombers under that heading. Seventeen fighters were lost. The total casualties inflicted on the Germans by all RAF warplanes were thirteen seamen killed and sixty-eight wounded. The Luftwaffe lost seventeen aircraft and eleven pilots.

Some minor injuries were suffered by the lesser German warships, not all of them caused by the British. Destroyer *Z-29*, for instance, was damaged when one of her anti-aircraft shells accidentally exploded. Her speed was reduced and Vice Admiral Ciliax and his staff transferred to another destroyer, the *Hermann Schoemann*, but the incident merely slightly delayed *Z-29*'s safe return to her homeland. The battle-cruisers, however, were less fortunate.

Ironically the greatest harm to befall the Brest Group occurred after all the British attacks had ceased. At 1955, *Gneisenau* struck a mine laid by RAF aircraft some days earlier. The explosion ripped a hole in her bottom and threw a propeller shaft out of line but she was soon able to resume a speed of 25 knots. *Scharnhorst* at this time was lagging well behind the main enemy force. At 2134, she also hit a mine in much the same area as her sister ship had done. Both her main engines and her steering gear were put out of action and she was flooded by 1,000 tons of seawater. For almost an hour she lay dead in the water but eventually managed to limp on at 12 knots. Both battle-cruisers and *Prinz Eugen* entered German harbours in the early hours of 13 February.

The completion of the Channel Dash was greeted with delight throughout Germany. Ciliax declared that: 'In spite of the damage sustained by *Scharnhorst* and *Gneisenau*, it can be said that the success achieved was above all expectations.' Galland considered that the operation constituted 'in planning and execution, a great and impressive victory'.

Only Grand Admiral Raeder remained sulkily unimpressed, describing the Channel Dash as 'a tactical success but a strategic defeat', an attitude later embraced eagerly in government and service circles in Britain. Certainly Bomber Command was delighted to cease those attacks on Brest that it felt had proved a distraction from its 'proper' task of raiding German cities. Certainly the Royal Navy was no longer faced with the need to guard against sorties by the battle-cruisers as well as the *Tirpitz*, but then the heavy units of the Home Fleet had already been and would continue to be tied down in northern waters watching the German units in Norway. Certainly the threat the Brest Group posed to the Atlantic convoys had been removed but then, as Hitler had pointed out, this would in any case only last while the warships at Brest remained undamaged.

In fact, Hitler would shortly be able to show a further justification for his attitude, though not one that would have given him much satisfaction. *Gneisenau* had been moved to the floating dock at Kiel where her injuries could be checked. On the night of 27/28 February, a raid by Bomber Command scored two direct hits on her. These killed ninety members of her crew and started a fire among the ammunition in the forepart of the battle-cruiser. The cumulative effects of the damage she had suffered – from the attacks on Brest, from the mine during the Channel Dash and from these latest bomb-hits – was such that it was estimated it would take a year to complete her repairs. In practice, other conflicting demands would mean that they were never completed.

Indeed, if Germany's 'strategic defeat' was less important than claimed in many later accounts, then equally her 'tactical success' would turn out to be less important than it first appeared. *Gneisenau* would never sail again; *Scharnhorst* was out of action for six months; only *Prinz Eugen* was in a fit state to proceed to Norway as Hitler desired. On 23 February, as she approached Trondheim she was torpedoed and badly damaged by submarine *Trident*. After making temporary repairs, she returned to Germany where she too remained out of action, in her case for eight months.

These mishaps to *Gneisenau* and *Prinz Eugen* of course only occurred later. Even the fact that both the battle-cruisers had been damaged by mines was not known in Britain when news of the Channel Dash became public on 13 February, and if it had been, it would have done little to reduce the outburst of anger, shock and humiliation that gripped the whole country. Churchill demanded an explanation from Admiral Pound. Curt and bitter signals were exchanged between the Admiralty and the Air Ministry and between the RAF's various Commands. Protest meetings were held, and in Parliament, members of all political parties joined in assailing the government and in particular the prime minister, who was only able to appease his critics by promising to set up a Board of Inquiry.

In his book *Fighter Command*, Air Marshal Sir Peter Wykeham notes, somewhat cynically, that: 'The British people are emotional about sea-faring matters, and this German effrontery, though it did them no immediate harm, disturbed them far more than the violation of their airspace by bombers that actually blew them to pieces.' Yet the general public had always accepted that it would be impossible to prevent all enemy aircraft from crossing the Channel. What they, and indeed world opinion in general, had never contemplated was that enemy warships would be able to defy British mastery of the seas and enter, let alone dominate the Channel without suffering immediate destruction.

On 14 February *The Times*, in a dignified and restrained leading article, suggested that the Brest Group had succeeded where the Spanish Armada had failed. It was not a very appropriate comparison, for the Armada had been intended to clear the way for an invasion while the Germans were intent only on escape. It also ignored the fact that the Armada had also moved through the Channel relatively unharmed and only afterwards, in a strange parallel with the Brest Group, did it suffer dire misfortunes. No-one, though, would quarrel with the newspaper's conclusion that: 'Nothing more mortifying to the pride of sea power has happened in home waters since the 17th Century.'

The Channel Dash, in short, shook British pride, British prestige, British confidence and the confidence of other nations in Britain. It inflicted a wound that rankled for a long time and perhaps never fully healed. The only good thing about it, apart from the courage and devotion to duty of individual service personnel, was that the rage and concern it aroused distracted attention from the next instalment of bad news that quickly followed it, although this was rightly called by Churchill 'the greatest disaster to British arms which our history records.'

Notes

1. Bomber Command was not exempt from the lack of success that attended so many British efforts in February 1942. That month saw only four major raids against targets in Germany, one of ninety-eight aircraft and the other three of about fifty each. They inflicted very little damage.

2. Beamish would shortly seek combat once too often. On 28 March 1942 he failed to return from a sweep over France and is believed to have been shot down by Messerschmitt Bf 109s.

3. Gleave had earlier seen service in the Battle of Britain, flying Hurricanes with 253 Squadron. On 30 August 1940 he shot down four Messerschmitt Bf 109s, all confirmed in German records, but the next day he was attacked in his turn by a 109. His Hurricane burst into flames and although he baled out, he suffered horrific burns to his face, hands and legs. After treatment from the noted plastic surgeon Archibald McIndoe that included giving him a new nose and new eyelids, he returned to active duty and took up his post at Manston in October 1941.

4. Mayer would go on to become one of the Luftwaffe's highest-scoring pilots in Western Europe, being credited with a total of 102 victories. He was killed in action on 2 March 1944.

5. The other members of 825 Squadron who lost their lives on this sortie were Sub-Lieutenants Parkinson, Fuller-Wright and Beynon and Leading Airmen Topping, Wheeler and Smith.

Chapter 5

Surrender at Singapore

In February 1942, bad news was received on the very first day of the month and it was ominous news too, foreshadowing the worst news of all that would soon come in from the same theatre of war. By 1 February, most of the British and Commonwealth units that had survived the fighting in Malaya had been withdrawn to Singapore Island and the great causeway, 1,100 yards long and 70 feet wide, connecting this to the mainland had been blown up, though the gap was only 4 feet deep at low tide and could easily be crossed. That is, most of the units, but not all of them.

Among those fighting in the Sultanate of Johore in the extreme south of the Malay Peninsula was 9th Indian Division. This had been retreating down a railway line, but at a village called Layang Layang, the road that had previously run alongside the tracks swung away from them. The division's artillery, transport and equipment, including its radios that were carried on trucks, needed to use the road and accordingly went south on this, but since it was also being used as the line of retreat for 8th Australian Division, the men of 9th Indian had to continue down the railway. It was planned that its two brigades should move back in succession through defensive positions held by the other one.

Therefore 8th Indian Brigade fell back from Layang Layang while 22nd Indian Brigade covered its withdrawal from defences set up just north of the village. Unhappily, 8th Indian moved back further than intended, enabling the very mobile Japanese to swing round into the gap between the two brigades and cut off 22nd Indian's line of retreat. To make matters worse, the premature demolition of a railway bridge also blew up the civilian telephone line that was now the only means by which 9th Indian Division could contact its isolated unit. The Divisional Commander, Major General Barstow, gallantly if unwisely set out on foot to make personal contact with his missing brigade, only to be ambushed by an enemy patrol and killed.

Attempts by 22nd Indian Brigade to break out of the trap and by 8th Indian to push north to its aid both failed, mainly because they had to be made without supporting artillery. Nor was there any chance of restoring communications between the two brigades. It was therefore reluctantly decided that 8th Indian at least must be brought back to the apparent safety of Singapore Island, while 22nd Indian made its escape as best it might. Brigadier Painter, unable to do so down the railway line, decided his one chance was to move his force through the jungle. Some sixty men did manage to reach the Johore Strait, across which small craft ferried them to Singapore. The main body of the brigade, however, hampered by their wounded, and exhausted and depressed by struggling through foul marshes swarming with insects, leeches and venomous snakes, were constantly harried by the Japanese. After four days and nights of torment, Painter bowed to the inevitable and on 1 February surrendered with 400 or so troops, all that remained under his command.

With this grim warning of what might be to come, the fight for the Malay Peninsula ended and the fight for Singapore Island became imminent. Churchill at least had no doubts about the action that should be taken. On 20 January, he had demanded prolonged resistance, culminating in street-fighting in Singapore City.

The officer to whom this message was sent was General Sir Archibald Wavell who, earlier in the month, had been appointed Supreme Allied Commander of ABDA, an organization with its headquarters in Lembang, east of Batavia (as the capital of Java was then known). From here it exercised theoretical control over all forces, American, British, Dutch or Australian – hence the initials of the Command – on land or sea or in the air, throughout a huge area of South-East Asia that included Malaya, Singapore, Burma, the Dutch East Indies, the Philippines and north-west Australia.

Wavell had seemed an ideal choice for the post of ABDA's Supreme Commander because as Commander-in-Chief, Middle East, he had been compelled to deal with campaigns not only in the Western Desert but in East Africa, the Balkans, Crete, Iraq and Syria. Yet wide as were the areas for which he had then been responsible, they were not as vast as those nominally under the control of ABDA. In practice, it was impossible for Wavell to direct the fighting in the Philippines, cut off and isolated by Japanese conquests, and very difficult for him to do so in Burma, situated at a huge distance from his HQ in Java.

Moreover, in the Middle East Wavell had enjoyed full authority over the separate areas under his command. In the Far East, he was subjected to numerous restrictions on his ability to intervene in matters considered the responsibility of the leaders of forces from nations other than Britain. Nor did it help that the ABDA countries all had very natural but very different priorities: the main wish of the Americans was to defend the Philippines, then an American colony; that of the British was to guard Singapore and Burma; that of the Dutch was to protect their East Indies; that of the Australians was to ensure there would be no invasion of Australia.

Nor, for all his fine qualities, was Wavell really suited for the task with which he had been entrusted. His immense responsibilities at times of great peril in the Middle East had exhausted him and he had been sent to take command in India partly at least to give him a chance to recover, only to find himself plunged into the heart of another conflict, conducted in even more desperate circumstances. Nor was his attitude towards the situation in Singapore very encouraging. On the one hand, he fatally underestimated the Japanese, admitting later that he did not 'appreciate what fine, brave and ruthless soldiers they were'. He therefore believed that resolute counter-attacks against them would solve any problem. On the other hand, he had no high opinion of the abilities of Percival or most of his subordinates and gloomily predicted that Singapore would be unlikely to hold out for long after the Malay Peninsula had been taken.

Percival, by contrast, appeared more sanguine. Reinforcements had been arriving at Singapore and although he did not believe the island could hold out indefinitely if unaided, he did hope that 'with firm resolve and fixed determination' it should be possible to resist until such time as 'the forces of the Allies' could 'be concentrated for this struggle in the Far East'.

To do so, Percival had 85,000 men, of whom 70,000 were fighting troops and the remaining 15,000 were on administrative duties.[1] There were sufficient supplies in Singapore to feed its garrison and civilian population for three months and the island's reservoirs could provide all the water needed if this was used with reasonable economy. The soldiers were also provided with all the ammunition they required apart from shells for their field artillery, and more than enough transport, fuel and medical equipment.

While the garrison's numbers were impressive on paper it suffered, however, from several practical disadvantages. Perhaps the most significant was that Singapore's fixed defences were all designed to meet an assault from the sea. It is frequently stated that none of its heavy guns could be traversed so as to fire on an attack coming over the Johore Strait. In reality, many were able to do so, including, it may come as a surprise to learn, all five of Singapore's heaviest 15-inch weapons. Unfortunately, because it had been envisaged that they would oppose enemy warships, they had all been supplied with armour-piercing shells and these were largely ineffective against a hostile army; high-explosive projectiles were needed to deal with this.

For the same reason, it was in the south and east of the island that defences like concrete pillboxes, anti-tank ditches and minefields were clustered. To the north and west even such limited obstacles as barbed-wire fences had hardly existed at the time of Japan's entry into the war and after it, there was a reluctance on the part of the authorities to rectify the situation for fear that this would damage morale and an even greater reluctance on the part of the local civilian labour to proceed with the necessary work under constant threat of attack from the dominant Japanese Army Air Force.

Then again, most of Singapore's fuel, supply and ammunition dumps were located in the north where they were at risk of an early capture in the event of an invasion from the mainland. On 1 February Japanese artillery opened fire across the Johore Strait against these targets and also on the airfields at Seletar, Sembawang and Tengah, all within easy range and already bombed repeatedly. By 3 February, all three had been rendered inoperable, leaving the RAF with only the civilian aerodrome at Kallang. This had been built on reclaimed land just east of Singapore City and it 'oozed mud through every bomb crater'. It was therefore decided to withdraw all RAF aircraft to Sumatra except for ten Hurricanes and six Buffaloes; these, on Percival's urging, remained at Kallang, where they gave some encouragement to troops and civilians alike.

Perhaps the greatest handicap imposed by the geography of Singapore Island, however, was the fact that, though it is nowhere more than 27 miles from east to west or 13 miles from north to south, its coastline is 70 miles long. Percival did not have enough men to guard such an area and since he believed his best chance of holding out was to destroy the Japanese on the beaches before they could establish themselves ashore, he was anxious to anticipate the place where they would land.

Both Wavell and Percival's own Intelligence staff had calculated that the invasion would come in the north-west of the island where the Johore Strait was narrowest. Percival, though, perhaps feeling that this was too obvious and having received reports of enemy transport moving into positions opposite to the north-east coast, believed that the assault would be launched here. He was fortified in his opinion by heavy enemy bombardments being delivered in this area and by the Japanese seizure on 7 February of an islet called Pulau Ubin that lay north-east of the main island. In the north-east, therefore, he placed his strongest formation: III Army Corps under Lieutenant General Sir Lewis Heath.

At the start of the campaign in Malaya, III Corps had been composed of 9th and 11th Indian divisions, each containing two brigades, and the independent 28th Brigade of Gurkhas. During the early fighting, however, both of 11th Division's brigades, 6th and 15th Indian, were so badly battered that by the end of December 1941, they had merged into a single unit with the rather unimaginative title of 6th/15th Brigade. The 11th Division was strengthened by the inclusion of 28th Brigade and of 12th Indian Brigade which had previously formed the Army Reserve. However, in early January 1942 12th Indian Brigade in its turn was so savagely mauled that its survivors had to be withdrawn from the front line to Singapore where the unit was reformed with the aid of newly-arrived and largely untrained reinforcements and 150 Marines who were survivors from *Prince of Wales* and *Repulse*.

Further calamities befell III Corps at the end of January: 6th/15th Brigade, forbidden to retire from a dangerously exposed position, was cut off by the Japanese. It was forced to abandon all its guns, transport and wounded and to make its way to the British lines in separate groups. Only one party of 1,200 men, guided by a Malay policeman, was able to reach these. Another 2,700 headed for the coast, whence they were evacuated to Singapore by two gunboats towing smaller craft in a series of transport missions, the last of which took place on 1 February. The remaining troops, including Brigadier Challen, fell into enemy hands.

Meanwhile, as recorded earlier, disaster had befallen III Corps' 9th Indian Division. With its commander Major General Barstow dead and its 22nd Indian Brigade annihilated, the division was dissolved and its remaining 8th Indian Brigade was transferred to 11th Indian Division. In the fight for Singapore, therefore, 11th Indian contained three brigades: 8th Indian, the remains of 6th/15th Indian and the Gurkha 28th Brigade, all stationed in the north-east of Singapore Island.

These units did not make up the full strength of III Corps, for on the right flank of 11th Indian was the recently-arrived 18th (British) Division. This had originally been intended for the Middle East, but had been hurriedly diverted. Its 53rd Brigade reached Singapore on 13 January to be greeted by a heavy, if not very effective, air-raid. The soldiers were not at all fit after a voyage of nearly three months, had had no training for action in the jungle and lacked any experience of combat of any kind. Nonetheless, the defenders of Malaya had already suffered so severely that the brigade was at once sent into action and endured heavy losses as a result.

The remainder of the division, 54th and 55th (British) brigades, only arrived at Singapore on 29 January. Their men also were unfit, untrained and inexperienced but, not having fought in Malaya, their spirit was probably higher than that of the rest of III Corps; its troops, having retreated so often, were starting to lack confidence in their ability to get the better of their opponents. The British brigades were accompanied by a squadron of light tanks. Unfortunately, these were obsolescent, badly in need of an overhaul and manned by crews who had not been properly trained in their use.

Equally unfortunately, 54th and 55th brigades were short of equipment since this had followed them on a slower convoy. The four ships in this were supposed to approach Singapore under cover of night, thus escaping the notice of Japanese aerial reconnaissance, but the elderly transport *Empress of Asia*, carrying the bulk of the brigades' rifles and automatic weapons, fell behind her companions. Early on the morning of 5 February, she was sighted by the enemy 7 miles south-west of Singapore. Dive-bombers attacked and scored several direct hits that forced her to beach on a nearby islet, blazing furiously. Rescue craft manned by naval personnel and civilian volunteers taking the place of their usual Malay crews who had deserted them saved most of her crew, but the flames were too fierce to be mastered and she and almost all her valuable cargo were lost.

Lieutenant General Heath also commanded five field artillery regiments and two anti-tank regiments. In the south of the island, Major General Keith Simmons took control of the fixed defences, which were manned by the 1st and 2nd Malayan brigades and the hastily-recruited members of the Straits Settlements Volunteer Force. As a central reserve, Percival had only the weak 12th Indian Brigade.

There remained only the western half of Singapore Island, stretching from the broken causeway in the north to the mouth of the Jurong River on the south coast. This was the responsibility of 8th Australian Division, its 27th Brigade holding a narrow front from the causeway to the Kranji River in the north-west, while its 22nd Brigade guarded the coast between the Kranji and the Berih River in the west. The Australians had fought well on the Malayan mainland but they too had lost heavily and had been weakened rather than strengthened by the arrival on 24 January of 1,900 reinforcements with less than a fortnight's training, some of whom had previously never so much as fired a rifle. Discouragement was beginning to set in and Major General Gordon Bennett, the

Australians' leader, as Percival anxiously observed, 'was not quite so confident as he had been up-country.'

In addition to its own brigades, 8th Australian Division controlled the 44th Brigade of 17th Indian Division. This division's 45th Brigade had reached Singapore early in January, and although as inexperienced and untrained as 53rd (British) Brigade had, like this, been sent into action without any preparation and had fared even worse. Before the end of the month it had been cut off from the other British and Commonwealth forces and broke away only at the cost of abandoning its wounded and destroying its guns and transport. Its officers had been made the prime targets of enemy snipers and so many had been killed, among them Brigadier Duncan, that the brigade could not be reformed during the remainder of the campaign. The 44th Indian Brigade had arrived at Singapore on 22 January and was still less experienced than the sister brigade that the Japanese had just destroyed.

Gordon Bennett placed 44th Brigade on his left flank, watching the area from the Berih to the Jurong River. There were wide gaps between the various posts set up by both the Australians and the Indians and these were patrolled by a group of lightly-armed, partly-trained but enthusiastic Chinese volunteers raised by Lieutenant Colonel John Dalley of the Federated Malay States Police, after whom they were known officially as 'Dalforce' and unofficially as 'Dalley's Desperadoes'. As further support, Gordon Bennett could call on three field artillery regiments and three anti-tank batteries.

One other preparation was made by Singapore's defenders; necessary but disheartening. It was decided to demolish the great naval base that had cost £60 million to build to prevent it falling into enemy hands. The dockyard staff had already been sent to Ceylon, though their commander, Rear Admiral Spooner, had remained in Singapore at the cost, it would transpire, of his own life. Now the installations were blown up, the stores removed and the great floating dock scuttled in Johore Strait. It seemed to many an admission of impending defeat.

While Percival, Heath, Simmons, Gordon Bennett and their subordinates were grimly preparing for the inevitable Japanese assault, in a room at the top of a tower in the Sultan of Johore's red-

Churchill at the controls of the flying-boat in which he returned from the Arcadia Conference with President Roosevelt in January 1942. He was unaware that Britain's – and his – darkest days lay just ahead.

Churchill's enemies had also been making plans: Rommel in conference with his staff. The officer in the centre, on Rommel's immediate right, is his Intelligence Chief, von Mellenthin.

The Panzer Mark III. Note its short-barrelled 50mm gun. This had less penetrative power than those of Allied tanks.

The Germans' real tank-destroyer was their magnificent 88mm gun.

A British Matilda tank is knocked out.

Field Marshal Kesselring visits North Africa to present decorations to those under his command. In February 1942, however, his main attention was directed towards Malta.

Kesselring's aerial bombardment of Malta enabled the Axis powers to get supply convoys through to aid Rommel. This one is escorted by a Junkers Ju 88 fighter-bomber.

Axis aircraft also attacked convoys to Malta: a British merchantman sinking while an Italian torpedo-bomber flies overhead.

The Brest Group. Top: *Scharnhorst*; middle: *Gneisenau*; bottom: *Prinz Eugen*.

Lieutenant Commander Eugene Esmonde (second from left) with members of his 825 (Swordfish) Squadron. There appear to be no photographs of Esmonde at the time of the Channel Dash action that resulted in his being awarded a posthumous Victoria Cross. This one was taken in 1941 and of those shown, only Leading Airman Johnson (far right) took part in the action and he also would not survive it.

A Fairey Swordfish torpedo–bomber in flight.

General Wavell and Air Chief Marshal Brooke-Popham who were Commander-in-Chief, India and Commander-in-Chief, Far East respectively at the time when the war with Japan began. Both badly underrated the strength and ability of their new enemy's armed services.

Australian reinforcements arrive at Singapore. These later ones were inadequately trained and equipped.

The opposing commanders at Singapore. Left: Lieutenant General Yamashita, head of Japan's Twenty-Fifth Army. Right: Lieutenant General Percival, head of Singapore's defenders.

Japanese infantrymen: brave, capable and ruthless.

As the danger to Singapore increased, attempts were made to evacuate military and civilian personnel, but several of the vessels used fell victim to Japanese naval or air forces.

Among the last vessels to leave Singapore was HMS *Li Wo*, an auxiliary patrol vessel and former Yangtze River steamer. She encountered a Japanese invasion fleet making for Sumatra and engaged this with a courage and determination that earned the admiration of her enemies and a posthumous Victoria Cross for her skipper, Lieutenant Wilkinson.

Hawker Hurricane fighters at P1 airfield near Palembang, Sumatra. The Allied airmen were hopelessly outnumbered, but then put up a gallant resistance before they were overcome.

Palembang and the Musi River, up which Japanese troops advanced in barges to the capture of the city.

Japanese carrier *Akagi*, flagship of Vice Admiral Nagumo at the time of the attack on Port Darwin.

Japanese-eye view of Port Darwin during the attack.

The most spectacular moment of the attack on Port Darwin: the freighter *Neptuna* blows up. In the foreground is the corvette HMAS *Deloraine*.

After the attack: all that was left of the *Neptuna* lies alongside the damaged wharf.

The opposing commanders in Burma.
Left: Lieutenant General Iida, head of
Japan's Fifteenth Army. Right:
Lieutenant General Hutton, head of the
Burma Army.

Japanese Sally bombers on their
way to attack Rangoon.

Major General Smyth VC, commander of 17th Indian Division.

Brigadier (later Major General) Cowan, Brigadier General Staff, 17th Division.

Japanese infantrymen close in on the Sittang River bridge, seen in the background.

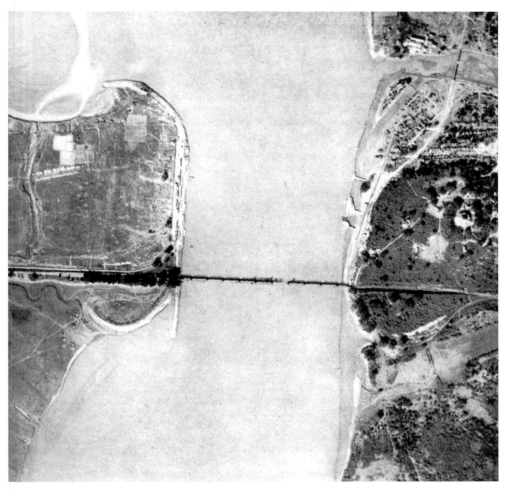

The Sittang River bridge. The gap that was blown in it, thereby trapping a large part of the 17th Indian Division, is clearly visible in this later aerial photograph.

Rear Admiral Doorman who commanded the ABDA Combined Striking Force in the Battle of the Java Sea.

Rear Admiral Tanaka who commanded a Japanese destroyer squadron in the Battle of the Java Sea.

The end of HMS *Exeter*: a photograph taken by a Japanese float-plane directing the fire of four enemy heavy cruisers.

brick, green-tiled palace, Lieutenant General Tomoyuki Yamashita, the head of Japan's Twenty-Fifth Army, was making his own plans. Yamashita had selected the palace because it gave an excellent view over the Johore Strait and he felt it would inspire his soldiers to know that their general was literally watching over their exploits. It was a somewhat risky choice, for the building was within easy range of British artillery fire but in practice Yamashita was in no danger since the British had never thought that their enemy would dare to use somewhere so conspicuous.

Yamashita had reason to feel confident. The succession of victories he had won in the Malay Peninsula was most encouraging. His preparations for the invasion had been thorough and meticulous. His preliminary moves had ensured he would have almost total command of the air and, although he did not yet know this, had diverted British attention to the north-east of Singapore Island while he intended to attack in the north-west.

Yet Yamashita did have his concerns. The quality of his soldiers was high, but not their numbers. His Twenty-Fifth Army was flattered by its title, for in size it was roughly equivalent to a British army corps. It contained just three divisions that between them could now muster a total of little more than 30,000 men. Captain Liddell Hart in his *History of the Second World War* states that there were two extra divisions from which the Japanese could be reinforced if needed but these formations, which wisely he does not identify, in fact existed only in the fearful imaginations of Singapore's defenders. Yamashita was thus not only heavily outnumbered but unable to replace any losses he might suffer.

During the campaign in Malaya, Yamashita's intention had been to move as fast as possible. In furtherance of that aim, his men had lived off the country, seizing any food they needed from the unhappy Malays, and they were so mobile that they had been able to seize the military supplies they needed as well since their swift outflanking tactics frequently took their opponents by surprise. These factors had enabled the Japanese to keep up constant pressure, but they were unlikely to be repeated in the fighting on Singapore Island and because of their reliance on them, the Japanese had largely outrun their own sources of supply.

Consequently, Yamashita and his supply officers were desperately eager to avoid a long struggle for Singapore. Above all, as Yamashita later admitted, he was 'very frightened' that he would be forced 'into disastrous street fighting'. In theory, therefore, Churchill's demand, later echoed by Wavell, for just such lengthy street-fighting was good advice from a purely military standpoint. Yet for humane reasons, it could scarcely be contemplated for it would result in the slaughter of Singapore's inhabitants whom it was the duty of the British to protect and the Japanese, whose Intelligence service was far better than that of the British, were well aware of this consideration.[2] Even without any street-fighting, however, a week's struggle on Singapore Island would in fact leave Yamashita very short of petrol and shells for his artillery, and his soldiers down to 100 rounds of small-arms ammunition each and two bowls of rice a day for food.

Despite his artillery shortages, Yamashita gambled on a heavy bombardment, intended to weaken the will of Singapore's defenders, as a preliminary to his invasion. Throughout 8 February, Singapore's supply and ammunition dumps were shelled, as were oil tanks, many of these being hit and releasing great palls of smoke to drift across the sky. After a brief lull at sunset, the bombardment was resumed with the main target now the defences manned by 22nd Australian Brigade where the Japanese planned that their invasion should take place.

For this Yamashita had allocated both the 5th Infantry Division of Lieutenant General Takuro Matsui and the 18th Infantry Division commanded by Lieutenant General Renya Mutaguchi. The 5th Division on the left flank of the landings employed three of its four regiments, keeping the fourth in reserve; 18th Division on the right had only three regiments available, the fourth having been sent to participate in the conquest of Borneo, and it used two-and-a-half of these in the attack with the remaining men as its reserve.

Under cover of the barrage, these troops scrambled into small boats that they had carried through the jungle to Johore Strait in order to achieve surprise. There were 300 craft in all: about 50 motor-boats, some 50 steel and timber pontoons and almost 200 collapsible launches with outboard motors that could carry 15 to 20 soldiers each or light artillery pieces if three of them were roped together. At 2230 the first of these, with 4,000 soldiers on board, neared the beaches, the mortars in the leading craft pouring down their fire on 22nd Australian Brigade.

The Australians were badly hampered in their attempts to thwart the landings by an unfortunate combination of circumstances. On their retirement to Singapore Island, their radio sets had been withdrawn for servicing and had not yet been returned to the forward companies. The artillery bombardment had cut their field telephone wires. They had, therefore, no means of requesting that searchlights in the area should illuminate the invaders and the crews of these had been instructed not to do so without express orders in case the searchlights should be destroyed prematurely. Nor could the defenders call on supporting fire from their own artillery batteries, and only a few of these opened up in response to signal flares.

Though the Australian machine-gunners inflicted heavy casualties on the invaders, small parties of these forced their way on shore and their numbers were rapidly increased as the little Japanese boats crossed and recrossed the Johore Strait to bring in later waves of attackers. By midnight, the Japanese had secured their bridgehead and an hour later, 22nd Australian Brigade and those Chinese volunteers who had tried to assist it were in full retreat, leaving behind a considerable number of prisoners whom the Japanese, unable to spare guards for them, tied up and left lying on the ground. Before dawn on 9 February, Lieutenant Generals Matsui and Mutaguchi – the latter with a bullet wound in the shoulder – some 23,000 of their men and a good deal of light artillery were all safely ashore.

Throughout the day, the Japanese continued to press home their advantage. For a start, their Army Air Force mounted attack after attack on British positions. By this time, the RAF force at Kallang had been reduced to just the ten Hurricanes which, despite the odds against them, kept up their hopeless resistance and during the day destroyed or damaged seven enemy aircraft for the loss of three British fighters. Next day, the seven surviving Hurricanes were ordered off to Sumatra. It was hoped that the RAF in the Dutch East Indies might continue to assist in the defence of Singapore, using Kallang as an advanced landing ground but, as Percival would later recall sadly, 'no British aircraft were seen again over Singapore.'

On land, both 5th and 18th Japanese Infantry divisions pushed forward towards the village of Ama Keng on the high ground near which 22nd Australian Brigade was attempting to make a stand. The 2/20th Australian Battalion, faced by the whole might of 5th Division, was thrown back with heavy losses; 18th Division broke through the defenders between 2/18th and 2/19th Australian battalions and then, turning left and right, threatened to cut off both of them. Brigadier Taylor hastily ordered all his men to retreat and by 1000, they were back on the abandoned Tengah airfield where they were joined by 2/29th Australian Battalion from 27th Brigade which Gordon Bennett had ordered up to support them.[3]

Gordon Bennett had hoped that this reinforcement would enable the Australians to counter-attack, but Brigadier Taylor quickly concluded that this would not be possible and, indeed, that his men were still dangerously exposed and should withdraw even further. He therefore left Tengah airfield which the Japanese occupied that evening, and fell back to the 'Jurong Line'. This was not a 'line' in the usual military sense, having few fixed fortifications, but it was a naturally good defensive position, being a high ridge of land running between the headwaters of the Kranji River in the north and the Jurong River in the south.

Taylor's retirement meant that 44th Indian Brigade, stationed south of 22nd Australian, could be outflanked, so it too was ordered back to the Jurong Line; a good move really because it was important that this be held as strongly as possible. It blocked the path of any Japanese advance westward and it protected the vital village of Bukit Timah. This was the site of the British army's main food depot and of a large petrol dump and from it a major road ran straight to Singapore City.

As darkness closed in on 9 February, Lieutenant General Yamashita came ashore on the original Japanese landing area and set up his advanced headquarters in a rubber plantation. He had also decided to bring in his third main formation, the Imperial Guards Division. Despite its impressive name and the fact that it contained the tallest men in the Japanese army, this contained only two complete regiments and one extra battalion from another regiment. In the conquest of Malaya it had played a less important part than

Yamashita's other divisions, had suffered heavy losses and had shamefully vented its spite on wounded and helpless prisoners. Yamashita rated it as poorly-trained and heartily disliked and was disliked by its commander, Lieutenant General Takuma Nishimura.

Nishimura's target was the area between the causeway and the Kranji River, held by 27th Australian Brigade. He intended to use one full regiment plus the additional battalion and keep his other full regiment in reserve. The invaders began to move over the Johore Strait at about 2030 in the boats that had previously carried the other divisions. Their movement had been preceded by a heavy artillery bombardment and this had again destroyed forward telephone lines, preventing the Australians from making full use of their own artillery and searchlights. By midnight, the Japanese had established a beachhead, though not without losses inflicted by the Australians' mortar and machine-gun fire.

Japanese casualties were increased by the unofficial action of Lieutenant Watchorn, an Australian sapper officer who had had orders to destroy the oil depot at Kranji. He opened the valves of the tanks, letting out the fuel to seep over the waters of the Strait. Then he ignited it, engulfing a number of landing craft in a lethal wall of flame.

This episode so alarmed Lieutenant General Nishimura that he suggested his attack be abandoned and his troops brought ashore on the beaches used in the original Japanese landing. Yamashita contemptuously ordered him to clarify the situation first. On doing so, Nishimura discovered that his men were still holding firm in their beachhead, so he resumed his attacks. At about 0430 on 10 February, 27th Australian Brigade began to fall back to the south-east. Brigadier Maxwell would later insist that he had had full permission to do so from 8th Australian Division's HQ, but Gordon Bennett would claim that no such approval had been given and that he did not even hear about this action until some hours later. Probably the Australians' poor communications had brought about this mutual misunderstanding.

In any event, Maxwell's retirement presented Singapore's defenders with a number of problems. It gave the Japanese control of the causeway and they immediately set to work to fill the gap in this so that they could use it to bring up their heavy artillery. It exposed the left flank of III Corps by abandoning to the enemy the village of Mandai on a strategically important crossroads; Lieutenant General Heath tried hard to recapture this throughout 10 February but was thwarted by typically stubborn Japanese resistance. Worst of all, it threatened the defenders' crucial position on the Jurong Line.

That this was the key to a successful defence was fully appreciated by Percival and during the night of 9/10 February, he sent every reinforcement he could find to support it. His only reserve formation, 12th Indian Brigade, was ordered to hold its northern sector. Brigadier Paris had under him only the 4th Battalion of the 19th Hyderabad Regiment and the 2nd Battalion, Argyll and Sutherland Highlanders to which had been added the Marines from *Prince of Wales* and *Repulse*. To strengthen him, therefore, Percival gave him 2/29th Battalion so recently sent to 22nd Australian Brigade.

To guard the centre of the line, Percival chose 6th/15th Brigade which he detached from III Corps and also the Special Reserve Battalion, newly formed from mainly administrative troops. This enabled the battered 22nd Australian Brigade to be pulled back and used as the Jurong Line's reserve force. Meanwhile, 44th Indian Brigade held the southern part of the line.

Although these moves, arranged in haste and carried out partly in darkness, were, perhaps inevitably, somewhat confused and chaotic, by the morning of 10 February Percival had reason to hope that the troops on the Jurong Line were now strong enough to put up a resolute defence. However, the events of that morning quickly shattered any such delusions. First, Brigadier Paris learned of the retreat of 27th Australian Brigade and realized that this had left the way wide open for the Imperial Guards Division to advance southwards directly on Bukit Timah. He therefore swung his 12th Indian Brigade back to the village of Bukit Panjang, north of Bukit Timah, where he could block such a move. Unfortunately, by so doing, he also deprived the northern part of the Jurong Line of its defenders.

Worse was soon to follow. On the previous evening, Percival had notified Gordon Bennett that if the Japanese broke through the

Jurong Line, he still planned to hold Bukit Timah as part of a wide defensive perimeter around Singapore City. This message had been marked 'Secret and Personal', indicating that it was only for the eyes of the officer to whom it was addressed. Gordon Bennett, though, ignored this instruction and on the morning of 10 February, circulated the information to his subordinates holding the Jurong Line. In the prevailing tense and uncertain atmosphere, most of them read this not as a possible future requirement but as a present intention to retire to the perimeter stated; an interpretation perhaps encouraged by the abrupt departure of 12th Indian Brigade.

Accordingly, 22nd Australian Brigade, which as the reserve unit could have filled the gap left by 12th Indian, retreated instead towards Bukit Timah and 44th Indian Brigade, already under fire, followed its example; 6th/15th Brigade and the Special Reserve Battalion, with both their flanks now open to attack, had no choice but to fall back also. These actions exposed the right flank of 1st Malayan Brigade holding the coast south-east of the Jurong Line and it withdrew as well.

Such was the unwelcome news that greeted General Wavell who now arrived at Singapore by flying-boat to see the situation for himself. He agreed with Percival that the Jurong Line-Bukit Timah area was crucial and both set off for the headquarters of 8th Australian Division near Bukit Timah to discuss the position with Gordon Bennett. Their conference was interrupted by an air-raid, during which one bomb hit the headquarters building. Luckily it failed to explode but Percival would long remember the 'unedifying spectacle' of three senior officers 'going to ground under tables, or any other cover that was available.'

Wavell was not impressed by what he had learned. He would advise Churchill that: 'Morale of some troops is not good and none is as high as I should like to see.' His forebodings would soon be justified as Yamashita followed up his successes. That evening, 5th Infantry Division, thrusting towards and to the north of Bukit Panjang, made contact with the Imperial Guards Division and routed 4/19th Hyderabads. The remainder of 12th Indian Brigade held firm for a time in and south of Bukit Panjang but the Japanese had at last managed to bring some medium tanks onto Singapore

Island and with their aid 5th Infantry Division overran first 2/29th Australian Battalion and then 2nd Argyll and Sutherland Highlanders. It then pressed on to Bukit Timah. To prevent the petrol depot near the village falling into enemy hands, Percival ordered it to be set alight; it burned for forty-eight hours. At about midnight, the Japanese captured Bukit Timah and with it supplies of food to mitigate their own shortages.

Also that night, Wavell left Singapore after instructing Percival to fight to the last and to begin by recapturing Bukit Timah. One final personal misfortune would befall ABDA's Supreme Commander. As he made his way in the dark to the launch that was to take him to his flying-boat, he stumbled off the quay and broke two small bones in his back. On his return to Java he had to be taken to hospital, where he remained for twenty-four hours.

Subsequent events did little more than provide an endless series of setbacks and disasters. The fighting around Bukit Panjang had resulted in 12th Indian Brigade ceasing to exist as an organized formation. The 6th/15th Brigade lasted only a little longer: trying to withdraw across open country south of Bukit Timah to Singapore City, it was attacked by the Japanese 18th Infantry Division at about 0300 on 11 February and after a number of clashes throughout the night, its retreat was cut off and it was virtually destroyed. The 22nd Australian Brigade was also engaged and suffered losses but managed to retire to Singapore in reasonably good order.

The same date (11 February) also marked Percival's last attempts to arrange the counter-attacks that Wavell had ordered. In the north, 27th Australian Brigade was instructed to make a further effort to take Mandai village, but it was slow to organize this and before it could complete its preparations it was assaulted by the Imperial Guards Division and driven back still further. This decided Heath to withdraw III Corps' 11th Indian Division from its most northerly positions around the naval base in order to avoid being outflanked.

A counter-attack was made by three British battalions that Percival had taken from 18th (British) Division. Known as 'Tomforce' from its leader Lieutenant Colonel Thomas, this unit made a valiant attempt to recapture Bukit Timah, but was thrown back by superior Japanese forces supported by artillery and by a dive-bomber raid. It retired to stand guard over the Pierce and MacRitchie reservoirs in the centre of Singapore Island. Here it was taken over by a larger hastily-arranged formation led by Brigadier Massy-Beresford, but on the 12th all the defenders of the reservoirs came under repeated attacks from 5th Infantry Division, backed by tanks, and were compelled to abandon them.

Before leaving Singapore, Wavell had arranged the immediate transfer of all RAF personnel to the Dutch East Indies, though Air Vice-Marshal Pulford, a great friend of Percival, had refused to go with them. Now on 11 and 12 February, Percival organized the evacuation by sea of as many wounded men and female nursing staff – British, Australian and Indian – as possible. Despite heavy bombing, most of the ships involved escaped safely but one, the *Vyner Brooke*, was sunk off Banka Island near the south-east coast of Sumatra. Most of her 300 passengers were drowned and those who managed to struggle ashore, including a number of nurses, were later massacred in cold blood.

Also on the 12th, Percival ordered all his formations to fall back to a final perimeter, 28 miles long, which contained little more than Singapore City and Kallang airfield; a move that was completed by midday. As mentioned earlier, Percival could have made the Japanese position difficult had he been willing to indulge in the street-fighting that Churchill and Wavell wanted, but he was not prepared to subject Singapore to this final horror and on the 13th he specifically advised Wavell, who in turn reported to the prime minister, that: 'There must come a stage when in the interest of the troops and civilian population further bloodshed will serve no purpose.'

Already, indeed, the inhabitants of Singapore were suffering greatly and their misery increased as the Japanese surrounded the city and bombed and shelled it repeatedly. Unburied corpses, abandoned vehicles and wreckage of every kind littered the streets. The loss or destruction of food and petrol depots had greatly reduced supplies of these and the shelling had fractured Singapore's precious water mains, allowing most of the water to drain away. Fires raged on all sides. On 11 February, the Indian Base Hospital in the north-west of the city had gone up in flames which spread so rapidly that only a few of the patients could be rescued in time. At Kallang, timber sheds were ablaze with flames reaching a height of 600 feet. Oil tanks on islets just south of Singapore were set alight by the British themselves to deny them to the enemy. It is estimated that the civilian population was now suffering 2,000 casualties every day.

Everywhere there were signs that morale was disintegrating. Officials were burning secret documents and reserves of paper money. Bottles of alcohol were being smashed because it was feared that if victorious enemy soldiers were to obtain them, they would get out of control and indulge in all kinds of atrocities. Most depressing of all was the sight of large numbers of soldiers who had deserted: some, probably shellshocked, were sitting about numbly waiting for whatever fate might send; others, more aggressive, were forcing their way onto the evacuation ships, stealing fishing boats, or looting shops at gunpoint.

At a conference of senior officers on the 13th, Heath and Gordon Bennett both advised Percival to surrender forthwith. He declined to do so, but that night he ordered the fifty small vessels still in Singapore harbour to leave, carrying trained officers and technicians who could be of use elsewhere and as many of the remaining nurses as possible. Only about ten of these were able to reach safety. The rest ran into powerful Japanese naval forces escorting transports preparing for an attack on Sumatra and were sunk or captured.

One of the ships lost was a naval patrol launch with about forty-five evacuees on board, including Rear Admiral Spooner and Air Vice-Marshal Pulford who had been specifically ordered by Percival to leave. Pursued by enemy destroyers, they were forced to run their little craft aground on an islet near Sumatra. Short of food and ravaged by fever, eighteen of them died, including both Spooner and Pulford. The rest, now led by Wing Commander Atkins, were discovered by the Japanese and carried off to a prison camp in Singapore.

It was just one more of the minor tragedies of February 1942, but the story was at least brightened by an act of particular gallantry. Among the vessels escaping from Singapore was the *Li Wo*, a 707-ton former Yangtze River steamer, now converted into an auxiliary patrol vessel. She was armed with a single old 4-inch gun for which she had less than forty shells plus a couple of machine guns, but on encountering the Sumatra invasion force on 14 February her skipper, Lieutenant Thomas Wilkinson, an officer of the Royal Naval Reserve, at once attacked, scoring hits on a transport that set her on fire. *Li Wo* was then seriously damaged by the gunfire of Japanese warships, and in a last defiant gesture Wilkinson rammed the transport he had hit in a vain attempt to finish her off. The two ships drifted apart and *Li Wo*, hit repeatedly, sank. There were only ten survivors and Wilkinson was not among them. After the war, on the testimony of admiring enemy officers, he was awarded a posthumous VC.

On Singapore Island on 14 February, there was no such incident to offer consolation for British misery. The Japanese had managed to repair the broken causeway and bring up their heavy artillery to increase their bombardment of the defences. All three Japanese divisions attempted to thrust into the city but succeeded only in the south-west, aided by Gordon Bennett who, in order to save ammunition, refused to allow his artillerymen to fire on enemy forces attacking the neighbouring 1st Malayan Brigade. This had a horrifying consequence, for the Japanese broke through to the Alexandra Military Hospital where, claiming that they had been fired at from its grounds, they slaughtered some 200 of its occupants, medical staff and patients alike.

Gordon Bennett in fact had become totally defeatist. He signalled to his government in Australia that if the Japanese entered the city behind his position, he would 'avoid any further needless loss of life' by surrendering. He did not convey this intention to Percival, who would later describe his behaviour, with considerable restraint, as 'a most extraordinary procedure'.

Percival still hoped to be able to hold out a little longer, but at 0930 on 15 February he received the devastating news that the water supply would last for only another twenty-four hours and if it failed could not be restored for several days. Heath and Gordon Bennett again advised, almost demanded, an immediate surrender, though it might be added that Gordon Bennett had no intention of 'going into the bag' personally. With two of his officers he escaped from Singapore in a junk, ultimately getting back to Australia. He claimed that his sole motive was to be able to warn his country of the calibre of her enemies, but the military authorities were most displeased that he had not remained with his men and a Court of Inquiry after the war declared that his action 'was not justified'.

For Percival, in any case, all hope had now vanished. A delegation bearing a white flag was sent to discuss terms of surrender. The Japanese demanded that Percival come to meet with Yamashita at the Ford Motor Factory near Bukit Timah. The British and Japanese army commanders met there at 1715. At 1810, Percival signed the formal document of capitulation.

Although this was officially described as 'unconditional', in fact Percival did his best to provide some protection for his troops and the civilian population. It was agreed that all fighting would cease by 2030 and the British troops would lay down their arms by 2130 apart from 1,000 men who might retain their weapons to prevent riots and looting. The Japanese agreed they would not enter Singapore until 16 February, to give time for the news of the surrender to become known. They observed this condition and on the 16th, only their tanks passed through the city on a 'Triumph Parade', while Japanese flags were hoisted on all public buildings. The bulk of Twenty-Fifth Army remained outside the city and there was no orgy of rape, murder and looting like the one that had followed the fall of Hong Kong.

The Japanese also promised to guarantee the lives of troops and civilians 'absolutely'. They did treat the Malays reasonably well and the British civilians suffered an imprisonment that was endurable, if not pleasant. Horrible atrocities were, however, committed against the Chinese, with whose country Japan had been at war since 1937, and total indifference was shown towards the sufferings of the British, Australian and Indian soldiers who were considered by their captors to have disgraced themselves by their surrender. How many were captured at Singapore must be a matter of dispute because estimates of the size of the garrison vary so widely. Total casualties, though, must have been at least 85,000 and the vast majority of these became prisoners, thousands of them to perish from disease, hunger and overwork.

For their part, the Japanese in the fighting on Singapore Island had lost 1,714 killed, 3,378 wounded and not one man taken prisoner. These were slightly higher casualties than they had suffered in the whole course of the campaign in the Malay Peninsula. It was still a small price to have paid for a valuable naval base, for Malaya's rubber and tin, and for inflicting on Britain her greatest ever military humiliation.

The immensity of that humiliation was summarized by Lieutenant General Sir Henry Pownall, who was Wavell's chief of staff: 'We were frankly out-generalled, outwitted and outfought. It is a great disaster for British Arms, one of the worst in history, and a great blow to the honour and prestige of the Army. From the beginning to the end of this campaign, we have been outmatched by better soldiers.'

Notes

1. These are minimum figures. Some sources claim that the correct numbers were 80,000 and 20,000 respectively.
2. On 11 February a Japanese aeroplane dropped a message addressed personally to Lieutenant General Percival. It warned him that any further resistance 'merely increases the danger to the million civilian inhabitants' – of Singapore – 'without good reason, exposing them to infliction of pain by fire and sword.'
3. The figure '2' included in the title of these and other battalions signified that this was the second time that the battalion in question had been formed as a unit in the Australian army.

Chapter 6

Destruction at Port Darwin

If the fall of Singapore made less of an impact on the general public in Britain than it should have done, it had a shattering effect on the general public in and perhaps even more on the governments of the Commonwealth countries, especially Australia. To the British, Singapore was an exotic location on the other side of the globe. To the Australians, as had been pointed out earlier by their then prime minister, Mr (later Sir) Robert Menzies: 'What Britain calls the Far East is to us the Near North.'

No-one, therefore, will fail to understand the mounting concern of Australia and, indeed, New Zealand as the list of Japanese conquests continued to lengthen, or their feeling that Churchill and his advisers had been far too complacent about both British weaknesses and Japanese strengths and so had failed to estimate correctly the threat posed by Japan. The reproaches of Mr Peter Fraser, Prime Minister of New Zealand, were frank but fair and received a sympathetic response from Churchill. Australia's Mr John Curtin, on the other hand, was extremely forthright, criticized some of Churchill's previous decisions, claimed with some justification that the Australians had better appreciated 'the trend of the Pacific situation' and generally adopted an attitude that Churchill considered unduly hostile.

Churchill was beset on all sides by bad news that reached its height in February 1942, and no doubt was also uneasily aware that it was by his decree that British strength in the Far East had been sacrificed for the sake of obtaining a victory in North Africa, one that had now proved indecisive and incomplete. He also had a long and unforgiving memory and, faced with Curtin's complaints, he was not prepared to forget that Curtin had turned down a suggestion from Menzies that Australia form a National Government similar to that in Britain – with Curtin as prime minister – and had preferred to concentrate all power in the hands of his own Labour Party that enjoyed a majority of two, had previously strongly approved Britain's policy of appeasement and had resolutely opposed conscription in Australia.

Consequently, while Churchill's signals to Curtin tried to offer reassurances and paid deserved tributes to Australia's fighting men, they also contained tart references to responsibilities for lack of war readiness and the fact that Britain but not Australia had imposed universal compulsory service. As the crisis mounted, the attitude of both prime ministers became ever more impatient, outspoken and confrontational. The crisis would pass, but the exchanges left such a bitter memory that fifty years later an Australian Prime Minister, Mr Paul Keating, could state, without a blush, that in 1942, Britain had 'decided not to defend the Malayan Peninsula, not to worry about Singapore and not to give us our troops back to keep ourselves free from Japanese domination.'

This breach was all the more sad because at the start of the war the two countries had been brought very close together by an Australian act of outstanding generosity. In 1931, the Statute of Westminster had recognized that the self-governing parts of the Commonwealth were nations in their own right, 'in no way subordinate one to another'. Nonetheless, in 1939, apart from the Irish Free State that remained neutral throughout and left the Commonwealth altogether in 1949, the Dominions rallied loyally to Britain's side, and first and foremost of them was Australia.

On 3 September 1939, the prime minister of Australia was Robert Menzies whose sincere belief was that, despite their independence, the Dominions were 'still members of one family, and our family feeling is reinforced rather than weakened by our adult growth.' Accordingly, when the invasion of Poland resulted in a British declaration of war on Germany, Menzies announced that 'as a result, Australia is at war.' He would accept no delay because he thought it would be 'intolerable' if the British people should be left to 'wonder whether they were standing alone'.

A second generous action quickly followed. On 15 September, Menzies called for volunteers for a Second Australian Imperial Force. By 1941 three divisions – 6th, 7th and 9th Australian – were serving with great distinction in the Middle East. Churchill was not one to overlook such gestures and although he and Menzies proved by no means in agreement on all matters, they remained good friends and Churchill would always express admiration for the Australian prime minister's courage and gratitude for his help.

One subject on which the two prime ministers disagreed was the extent of the threat posed by Japan. On 27 September 1940, that country had joined with Britain's enemies, Germany and Italy, in the Tripartite Pact. Since Japan deeply resented British support for her own enemy, China, and particularly the flow of supplies being sent over the Burma Road,[1] there was always a possibility that she might come into the Second World War on the side of her Axis partners. Should that happen, Australia would inevitably be involved and at a time when her finest fighting men – and also, incidentally, the 2nd New Zealand Division – would be overseas.

To any who expressed anxiety about such a scenario, the British government offered reassuring promises that protection for Australia and New Zealand would be provided by the Royal Navy and by the impregnable bastion of Singapore: these between them would hold the Japanese back at a safe distance. It seems clear that it was also anticipated that any move by Japan against Australia or New Zealand or even Singapore would not be tolerated by the Americans and would be opposed by the US navy as well.

Menzies was more doubtful of the chances of American intervention and of the ability of Singapore to defend itself successfully. In January 1941 he set out to visit first Singapore, then the Middle East and finally Britain, returning home only in May. During a lengthy stay in London he urged more than once that Singapore should be strengthened. As we have seen, Churchill's military chiefs shared his view but although during August and September 1941 the Australians sent their 8th Division, again a volunteer force, to join the garrison of Singapore, Churchill sent all his own available reinforcements to the Middle East instead, in his determination to gain a victory that would 'rank with Blenheim and with Waterloo'.

So when the Japanese onslaught exploded in all its fury upon the Allied nations, the Australians had every justification for feeling that the British government had failed miserably in its assessment of the danger. They had no justification whatever for suggesting or implying that the British government was indifferent to their plight, for it would make numerous attempts to rectify its mistakes and meet Australia's wishes, even if some of them were clumsy and inept. Had Menzies still been prime minister, it seems very probable that the mutual respect between him and Churchill would have prevented or at the very least much reduced the bad feeling that arose between their respective countries. Unfortunately, Menzies no longer held that office and the reason for this in itself ensured problems for the future.

When Menzies returned to Australia in May 1941, he found that his long absence had been and had made him personally very unpopular. Curtin's Labour Party opposed a vote approving his visit to London and he was forced to promise that he would not go abroad again without the consent of all parties in the Australian parliament. It was felt that he had become too compliant with the wishes of the British government. His decision that Australia was automatically at war with Germany 'as a result of' Britain's declaration of hostilities had aroused no objection in parliament or the newspapers at the time, but it was now considered that by making it, he 'had abandoned Australia's independent status as a nation'. Even his fellow ministers had come to regard him as a liability, and on 28 August he resigned and was succeeded as prime minister by Mr (later Sir) Arthur Fadden who had acted as his deputy during his absence.

Thereafter, Churchill found that relations with the Australian government had become more difficult. This was almost inevitable because no future Australian government would dare to risk accusations of being subservient to London. On the contrary, it would be eager to demonstrate its independence by declining to meet British wishes and, sadly, an opportunity to do this would not long be delayed.

Since April 1941 Major General Leslie Morshead's 9th Australian Division had been holding firm in the isolated Cyrenaican port of Tobruk, denying this to Rommel and presenting a permanent threat and handicap to his supply lines. The task was difficult, dangerous and unpleasant, and though it had been performed with matchless skill and courage, it was natural that the Fadden government should wonder whether their soldiers could continue to hold out under determined attack. In addition, it was desired that all Australian troops in the Middle East should be collected into a single Australian force to emphasize that they were not 'British' but allies of Britain, responsible to their own home government.

Accordingly, the Fadden administration requested that 9th Australian Division should be withdrawn from Tobruk. One of its brigades was duly replaced by 1st Polish Brigade but General Auchinleck was alarmed by air attacks on the ships involved and feared that any further missions would result in delaying his plans for Operation CRUSADER, success in which would ensure the relief of Tobruk in any case. He therefore urged that the rest of the Australians be allowed to remain where they were. Churchill in turn made similar representations to Fadden but without success.

Then on 6 October, the Fadden government was defeated in a vote on the Budget and Mr Curtin took office as prime minister. On the 14th, Churchill repeated to Curtin his appeal that any further replacement of 9th Australian Division be postponed until after CRUSADER – which, it may be recalled, would begin on 18 November – and expressed his confidence that this would not expose Morshead's men to any great danger. Curtin was adamant in his refusal, and during the remainder of October the Royal Navy ferried 70th (British) Division to Tobruk and took out the remaining Australians.

Churchill was not pleased by having to conduct risky operations that he believed, not without reason, were unnecessary. His displeasure was in no way diminished by the loss of the fast minelayer *Latona*, sunk by German aircraft on 25 October, or by having to mollify an aggrieved Auchinleck whose dignity had been affronted by what he considered was the lack of confidence in him shown by the Australian government. It was not a happy start to the relationship between Churchill and Curtin and it came at a time when tension with Japan was reaching breaking-point.

It must be clearly stated that the British government, far from deciding not to defend Malaya and not to worry about Singapore, was already becoming worried about both and taking active steps to defend them should this prove necessary. On land, the plans included one, called Operation MATADOR, to advance into neutral Thailand and seize the ports of Singora and Patani where it was correctly assumed the Japanese would land; an action that had been suggested by Menzies among others. At sea, Churchill sent a powerful striking force to Singapore that he hoped would deter Japan from commencing hostilities or destroy any invasion forces if she did.

That these hopes were not fulfilled in no way alters the sincerity of Britain's aims. Operation MATADOR failed because the British would not violate Thailand's neutrality until Japanese intentions had become clear beyond argument. As a result, the enemy, who had no such scruples, got to Singora and Patani first. Force Z, as Churchill's naval deterrent was known, was originally intended to include three major warships. Battleship *Prince of Wales* and battle-cruiser *Repulse* reached Singapore on 2 December, but were unaccompanied by aircraft carrier *Indomitable* which had been seriously damaged by running aground on a badly-charted reef.[2] After the deterrent had failed to deter, *Prince of Wales* and *Repulse* did attempt to defend Malaya by seeking out Japanese invasion convoys, only to be sunk themselves by enemy aircraft.

Their loss, following hard on the crippling of the American Pacific Fleet at Pearl Harbor, gave Japan temporary command of the seas. It caused dismay in Britain but consternation in Australia. Two of her promised safeguards, the protection of the Royal Navy and the intervention of the United States navy, had now vanished. There remained Singapore but this was obviously threatened as the Japanese forces in Malaya continued their relentless advance southward. No wonder Australians were alarmed.

Australia's prime minister was particularly alarmed and his reactions appeared more frenzied than considered. To both Churchill and Roosevelt, Curtin suggested that Australia might call for aid from Russia. Since Russia was herself having to receive war material from Britain and the United States, was a neutral in the war with Japan and anxious to remain one, and was separated from Australia by the Japanese conquests, neither the British prime minister nor the American president found this idea very impressive or meaningful. Curtin also called on America for support and protection. This was much more realistic but unfortunately in a signed newspaper article on 27 December, Curtin, himself a former journalist, declared that in the direction of the Pacific War, 'the United States and Australia must have the fullest say' and made it 'quite clear that Australia looks to America, free of any pangs as to our traditional links to the United Kingdom'.

Since this statement reaffirmed Australia's independence from Britain only to admit to a dependence on America, it was resented by many Australians and not well received in London or, perhaps surprisingly, in Washington. It was both uncalled-for and unnecessary. Churchill, as we have seen, did not exactly pour oil on troubled waters in his signals but he could truthfully contend that he was doing his best to meet Australia's natural wishes and relieve her natural anxieties.

Soon after Japan's entry into the Second World War, Churchill and his service advisers had travelled to America in the new battleship *Duke of York* and from 22 December 1941 to 14 January 1942 they held a series of discussions, collectively called the Arcadia Conference, with Roosevelt and his advisers. Churchill strongly put forward the need to help Britain's Dominions and the Americans generously agreed to take on a number of responsibilities including sending warships to the South-West Pacific to help defend the coasts of Australia and New Zealand and securing Pacific islands on the lines of communication to them. These moves would take time but as early as Christmas Day 1941, Churchill was able to telegraph the good news to Curtin. This, be it noted, was two days before Curtin saw fit to publish his contentious newspaper article.

Churchill thus clearly had every desire to keep Australia free from Japanese domination and he was very willing that Australia's own troops should take part in her defence. It will suffice to refer to a signal from Curtin to Churchill dated 11 January 1942 which confirms that agreement had been reached between them as to 'the dispatch of the 6th and 7th Australian Divisions, together with corps troops and maintenance and base organizations, from the Middle East to the Netherlands East Indies', the intention being of course that the

Japanese would be held as far away from Australia as possible.

Curtin certainly had every right to request the return of Australia's experienced soldiers, though it seems a pity that he could not bring himself to express even a formal pleasure that his request had been granted.[3] Yet neither this nor his declared reliance on America stopped him from reiterating his demands that Britain offer more resistance to the Japanese, mingled with acid comments on her previous unsuccessful attempts to do so. In his message of 11 January, for instance, he reminded Churchill that 'the Japanese have been able to overrun so easily the whole of Malaya except Johore', noted sardonically that 'the task of fighting the decisive battle' in Johore was to be given to 8th Australian Division and insisted that 'nothing be left undone to reinforce Malaya to the greatest degree possible.'

Churchill did his best. By 21 January, when it was clear to the most optimistic that the battle for Johore had been lost, he had sent out as reinforcements 17th Indian Division's 45th Brigade, 18th (British) Division's 53rd Brigade, an anti-tank regiment, one heavy and one light AA regiment and fifty Hurricanes in crates. All these units had taken part in the fighting and all had suffered accordingly.

Other reinforcements, chiefly 44th Indian Brigade and the two remaining brigades of 18th (British) Division, were also on their way to Singapore but by 21 January Churchill, who had been deeply disturbed by pessimistic reports from Wavell, was starting to wonder whether they should be allowed to proceed there and, indeed, whether it might not be best to transfer forces away from Singapore to Burma, a colony rich in oil and containing the Burma Road, the last remaining supply route to China.

On the 21st, therefore, Churchill wrote to his chiefs of staff to query if it might not be better for the British to blow up the docks and other vital installations at Singapore and to concentrate all efforts 'on the defence of Burma and keeping open the Burma Road'. He accepted that this would be an 'ugly decision', but feared that if it were not taken, Singapore and the Burma Road might both be lost.

Faced with such a dilemma, the British chiefs of staff understandably required time for consideration and before any conclusion could be reached, the matter was complicated by a particularly violent telegram from Curtin. In fairness to him, it should be pointed out that reports of Churchill's attitude had reached him hard on the heels of news of another Japanese success that appeared comparatively minor when viewed from London but was very serious in Australian eyes.

North of Australia, the huge 1,000-mile-long island of New Guinea was a mere 60 miles distant at its closest point but its towering, jungle-clad mountains placed a tremendous natural obstacle between Australia and any potential invader. To the north-east, however, lay the Australian-controlled islands of New Britain and New Ireland with magnificent harbours at Rabaul and Kavieng respectively. These, especially the former, would provide the Japanese with bases from which they could outflank the New Guinea barrier by dominating the Coral Sea, the south-west of which is bordered by the coast of Queensland. On 23 January, following a series of strikes by carrier-based aircraft, Japanese invasion forces did secure both Rabaul and Kavieng.

That evening, Curtin fired off his telegram. It followed a pattern that must have become unwelcomingly familiar to Churchill. There was a criticism of past actions: 'The trend of the situation in Malaya and the attack on Rabaul are giving rise to a public feeling of grave uneasiness at Allied impotence to do anything to stem the Japanese advance.' There was a reproachful reminder of benefits received: 'The Australian people, having volunteered for service overseas in large numbers, find it difficult to understand why they must wait so long for an improvement in the situation when irreparable damage may have been done to their power to resist.' There was a demand: he expected 'a flow of reinforcements'. There was, this time, a warning that came very close to a threat: 'After all the assurances we have been given the evacuation of Singapore would be regarded here and elsewhere as an inexcusable betrayal.'

Churchill was later to state, rather generously, that this message did not decide the issue and it is true that he still could have and, it has been argued, should have ended the 'flow of reinforcements' to Singapore. In reality, though, he could hardly expose his government to a charge of betrayal, especially wounding to a man of his temperament, from another member of the Commonwealth and one that had rendered splendid services to Britain. At the very least, Curtin's attitude did not encourage Churchill to make his 'ugly decision'. The planned reinforcements were duly sent to Singapore and to their destruction.

So to February 1942 and the seemingly endless series of misfortunes that shook even Churchill's resolution. There was plenty of bad news from the Far East besides that from Singapore during the early part of the month, and while this added to Churchill's burdens, it must have inflicted still more severe blows on Curtin and on the Australian people as a whole.

On 3 February the Japanese made their first air-raid on Port Moresby, an Australian air base and planned future army base on the southern coast of New Guinea. It caused little damage but another raid two days afterwards destroyed three Catalinas and damaged a fourth. There were further minor attacks later and though again they did not do much harm, they emphasized that the war was coming dangerously close to Australia.

What made this still more worrying was that Australian manpower was being steadily whittled away. An Australian unit of 1,090 men, coming mainly from 2/21st Battalion and known as Gull Force, had been sent to strengthen the Dutch on Amboina, a small but strategically important island that contained a vital airfield. The Australian CO, Lieutenant Colonel Roach, had protested that his men could not hope to prevent a Japanese attack, but the only step the authorities had taken was to relieve him of his command. Now his warning proved justified. On 2 February the Japanese captured the aerodrome, sending their aircraft to it three days later. On 4 February, organized resistance ceased and Gull Force passed into captivity.

Then on 8 February the Japanese moved to complete their conquest of New Britain by a landing at Gasmata in the south of the island. By the 9th, the target had been secured and the remaining men of New Britain's Australian garrison – 1,400 strong and coming chiefly from 2/22nd Battalion – were taken prisoner. These surrenders were quickly followed by the largest capitulation of all at Singapore on the 15th when the entire 8th Division disappeared from the roll of the Second Australian Imperial Force.

No sooner had the Australians learned that they could no longer rely on one bastion that they had thought would protect them than they were told they could no longer rely on another one either. By mid-February Borneo and Celebes were in Japanese hands, but the Australians still hoped that their enemies might be held at a distance by a successful defence of that chain of Indonesian islands, the chief of which were Sumatra, Java, Bali and Timor, that stretched away to the north-west of Australia's northern coast.

It was for this reason that Churchill and Curtin had agreed that 6th and 7th Australian divisions should help to defend the Dutch East Indies; they were to be stationed in Java and Southern Sumatra respectively. Unhappily, they would not become available until late March. In the meantime, another small Australian detachment, Sparrow Force, had been sent to Timor, the island closest to Australia, owned at this time partly by the Dutch and partly by the Portuguese. The 2/40th Battalion from Tasmania was based at Koepang, capital of Dutch Timor, while 2/2nd Independent Company, a commando-type unit of 340 men, joined a small Dutch detachment at the Portuguese capital of Dili.[4] On 15 February four transports carrying reinforcements left for Timor, but next day they were attacked, although without success, by Japanese aircraft and when it was learned that strong enemy naval forces were in the vicinity, ABDA Headquarters ordered their return to Australia.

Until the two Australian divisions could arrive, the ground defence of the remainder of this island barrier had to be left to the Dutch, but a small number of Allied aircraft had been sent to Java and a larger number to southern Sumatra where they operated from two airfields: P1 just north of Palembang, Sumatra's capital and centre of her oilfields; and P2, a secret base hacked out of the jungle some 20 miles to the south. In theory, Air Commodore Hunter, who commanded 225 (Bomber) Group, could call on the services of four squadrons of RAF Blenheims and one squadron of RAF and two of RAAF Hudsons, but all had been much reduced in size and the total number of his warplanes was only forty-eight. Air Commodore Vincent's 226 (Fighter) Group was made up of just 232 and 258 Squadrons, both equipped with Hurricanes.

These units did not escape the troubles suffered by all British forces in this dreadful month. Both the airfields had appalling landing surfaces and lacked proper facilities, accommodation and transport. Although the ground crews under Flight Sergeants Slee and Barber toiled heroically to cope with an almost total absence of tool kits and spare parts, it was normal for two-thirds of the twin-engined aircraft to be unserviceable and even the sturdy Hurricanes could rarely show as many as half their number ready for action.

In consequence, the British airmen were always desperately outnumbered and, just to increase their difficulties, they were never able to receive warning of enemy attacks for there were no radar sets in Sumatra and the Observer Corps posts were distributed far too widely. Thus on 4 February, the Hurricanes on P1 had hardly taken off when they were engaged from above by a swarm of enemy fighters and nine of them were shot down or crash-landed. On the 5th, a larger raid destroyed three Hurricanes and six Blenheims on the airfield, another three Hurricanes that had just taken off and one more Blenheim that was coming in to land.

Though improved radio communications brought better results against later raids, the RAF units in Sumatra were already very weak when, on 13 February, a reconnaissance Hudson sighted twenty-two transports, strongly escorted,[5] and carrying two regiments of Japan's 38th Infantry Division that had earlier been responsible for the capture of Hong Kong. Next day, part of this force seized Banka Island where 10 per cent of the world's tin was produced and, of more immediate value to them, where there was an aerodrome at Muntok. The main enemy convoy, meanwhile, moved on to the mouth of the Musi River on which Palembang stands. It was attacked by Blenheims and Hudsons but these inflicted much less damage than was believed at the time.

Unhappily, ABDA Headquarters in Java had ordered that the bombers be protected by every available Hurricane, contrary to the wishes of Air Commodore Vincent who believed his fighters should be held back to guard their own bases. His judgement was quickly proved correct, as the Japanese now sprang another surprise: 300 paratroopers were dropped at the oil refineries at Pladjoe just outside Palembang and 350 more close to the P1 airfield. The RAF personnel under Wing Commander Maguire put up a gallant resistance but were eventually compelled to destroy a number of unserviceable Hurricanes on the ground and abandon the aerodrome.

The airmen's fight was not yet over, however. They still retained their secret airfield at P2 and on 15 February, when the Japanese ground troops, who had now transferred to barges, pushed up the Musi River to Palembang, the Blenheims of 84 and 211 Squadrons and the Hudsons of 62 Squadron made repeated attacks on them. The remaining Hurricanes were even more effective. Flown alternately by pilots of each of their two squadrons so as to keep up constant pressure, they strafed the landing barges from very low level, causing casualties that ran into hundreds and long remained a grim memory with the Japanese units affected. They also raided Muntok aerodrome and destroyed a number of enemy warplanes on the ground.

If this episode provided a sad reminder of what might have been achieved had larger numbers of modern aircraft been sent to the Far East, in the present circumstances it could do no more than delay the Japanese advance. Aided by another paratroop landing, they captured Palembang on 16 February, and although P2 had remained undiscovered, it was decided that its situation had become untenable. By the 18th all surviving warplanes had left for Java where they would continue their hopeless fight until they were wiped out, while the ground crews sailed from the port of Oosthaven in the extreme south-east of Sumatra. In the confusion, large quantities of vital equipment such as spare Merlin engines for the Hurricanes were left behind. Fortunately, the effects of this action were mitigated by Group Captain Nicholetts who on 19 February returned to Oosthaven with a party of fifty volunteers to spend twelve hours salvaging as many stores as possible, unhindered by the enemy.

Nothing, though, could mitigate the effects of the loss of Sumatra. General Wavell on 13 February had already warned Churchill that its retention was 'essential for successful defence of Java' and sowed the seeds of further unpleasantness by suggesting that consideration should be given to the 'destination of the

Australian Corps', by which he meant 6th and 7th Australian divisions that together formed I Australian Army Corps. On the 16th, when it was obvious that Sumatra would not be retained, Wavell at least made it clear what should not be the Australian divisions' destination by declaring that 'efforts should not therefore be made to reinforce Java.'

With Sumatra gone and Java in effect 'written off', all Australian hopes that the islands of the Dutch East Indies would present a barrier between them and the Japanese were dashed, and the country's morale was further tried by the events that quickly followed. On 19 February the Japanese seized Bali and in the early hours of the 20th they invaded Timor. Dili fell after only token resistance and its defenders retired into the island's interior, from which they waged a guerrilla campaign for several months before being evacuated by submarine; at no time, though, did they challenge the enemy's supremacy. The Tasmanian battalion in Dutch Timor resisted the invaders until the 23rd, when they were finally overcome. A few individuals were able to escape by sea, but another 1,137 Australians were added to those already in Japanese captivity.

Relations between Britain and Australia were embittered still further by an appallingly misguided decision on the part of Wavell. On the 19th the fast transport *Orcades* reached Java, carrying the first contingent of Australian troops from the Middle East, 2/2nd Pioneer Battalion (which had, in fact, served as an infantry unit) and 2/3rd Machine-Gun Battalion. Despite having said that reinforcements should not go to Java, Wavell persuaded a reluctant Lieutenant General John Lavarack, the commander of I Australian Corps, to allow these formations to remain there to assist the Dutch. Two British anti-aircraft units and a squadron of light tanks of the 3rd Hussars were added to their strength and all were together named Black Force after the Australian commander, Brigadier Blackburn.

It is easy to understand the anger of the Australian government at this action, for all it achieved was to guarantee the loss of more of their soldiers. When Java was invaded, Black Force would face an entire Japanese division and the inevitable result can be summed up in the Australian casualty list: 36 killed, 60 wounded, 2,736 prisoners of war. This was virtually Wavell's last decision as Supreme Commander of ABDA. With Java now isolated, the Command, as everyone realized, had become a farce and at 0900 on 25 February it was formally dissolved and Wavell left by air to resume his post as Commander-in-Chief, India.

Australian anger was fuelled by Australian anxiety. On 19 February at Port Darwin, capital of the Northern Territory, the war, for the first time, reached the Australian mainland. It was brought there by a formidable foe: four of the same aircraft carriers, the airmen of which had delivered the attack on Pearl Harbor.

The originator of the raid on Port Darwin was Rear Admiral Tamon Yamaguchi, an extremely aggressive character who, during the Pearl Harbor operation, had commanded a division built around carriers *Soryu* and *Hiryu*. On the voyage home, Yamaguchi's force had been detached to support an assault on Wake Island, the American garrison of which had thrown back an earlier attempted landing, sinking two Japanese destroyers. After assisting in Wake's capture, *Soryu* and *Hiryu* had taken part in several operations in the Dutch East Indies, at Amboina for instance, and Yamaguchi recommended the attack on Port Darwin because this was the main Allied base from which the East Indies could receive supplies and reinforcements.

Yamaguchi's superiors accepted his proposition but, rather to his annoyance, decided that it would be best not to entrust the operation solely to his vessels but to the larger carriers *Akagi* and *Kaga* as well, thereby placing Yamaguchi, as at Pearl Harbor, under the command of Vice Admiral Chuichi Nagumo. On 19 February, all four carriers and their escorting warships were in the Timor Sea north-west of Port Darwin. At 0845, 81 Kates, capable of carrying torpedoes but on this occasion used as high-level bombers, 71 Val dive-bombers and 36 Zero fighters led, again as at Pearl Harbor, by the redoubtable Commander Mitsuo Fuchida, left on their mission of destruction.

Port Darwin was sadly unprepared, both morally and materially, for its coming ordeal. Isolated in the extreme north of Australia, it had no rail links and only very poor road links with the rest of the continent. It was suffering from shortages of food, drink including alcohol, and particularly petrol. Most of the civilian population had been evacuated by sea, leaving only 2,000, of whom just sixty-three were women, chiefly nurses and Post Office employees. Army and navy personnel were bored, exhausted by the tropical climate, and low in morale. The former at least were also on the worst of terms with the locals, having disgraced themselves by outbreaks of rioting and disorder.

Nor were Port Darwin's defences likely to present too much of a problem for Fuchida's veterans. Its radar was inoperable. Its anti-aircraft guns were widely scattered, short of ammunition, unsuitable for dealing with low-level attacks and manned by largely untrained crews. Its only fighter defence was a squadron of ten American Kittyhawks under Major Floyd Pell, and even they were only present on 19 February by accident: they had taken off intending to fly to Java via Timor, but had turned back when bad weather was reported.

Once more as at Pearl Harbor, the attack achieved complete surprise though, as at Pearl Harbor, the defenders received warnings that were disregarded. Australia's Department of Defence had set up a chain of observers, called coastwatchers, by the simple method of equipping volunteers in offshore islands with radio sets and instructing them to report the movements of any ships and aircraft that they sighted. North of Port Darwin were Melville and Bathurst Islands and at 0915 John Gribble, the coastwatcher on Melville, and at 0937 Father John McGrath at the Roman Catholic Sacred Heart Mission on Bathurst reported the Japanese raiders. Unfortunately, there had been a number of false alarms in the past and RAAF Intelligence dismissed the reports, apparently believing that the aircraft sighted were Pell's Kittyhawks.

In an attempt to achieve surprise, Fuchida took his men on a wide sweep east of Port Darwin and attacked from landward. As a result, the Japanese aircraft were first sighted by an AA post on the heights overlooking the harbour. Lieutenant Robertson correctly identified them as hostile and at 0957 sounded the alarm. Like Rear Admiral Bellinger at Pearl Harbor, he added: 'This is no drill.' He then followed up with an authentic Australian confirmation: 'This is fair dinkum.'

By that time, one of Fuchida's pilots had already seen action.

Near Bathurst Island, the Japanese spotted two small American freighters, the *Don Isidro* and the *Florence D*. These were manned by Filipino crews who were attempting to take supplies to their home islands. Above them a US Catalina flying-boat was circling protectively and one Zero pilot, Petty Officer Yoshikazu Nagahama, promptly engaged this, setting one of its engines on fire. Its pilot, Lieutenant Thomas Moorer, managed to ditch his machine and he and his crew were rescued by the *Florence D*. Their adventures, however, were not yet over.

Nor were those of Nagahama. He had now lost contact with the rest of his formation, so he proceeded to Port Darwin alone and was in fact the first Japanese pilot to arrive. Pell's Kittyhawks had just returned from their abortive sortie and the leader and four of his men had landed to refuel. The remaining five, led by Lieutenant Robert Oestreicher, stayed on patrol overhead and Nagahama, sighting these below him, attacked them single-handed. Oestreicher, the only experienced pilot, took evasive action and later landed safely after engaging the main Japanese formation, but Nagahama shot down three Kittyhawks, killing Lieutenants Peres and Perry, and so damaged a fourth that it crashed on landing and was written off.

Major Pell and the four pilots with him tried to take off as the main enemy wave came in, but were strafed by Zeros as they did so. Lieutenant Hughes was killed and Pell was forced to bale out at only 70 feet, his parachute just opening in time. He was still badly injured when he hit the ground and was finished off by low-flying Zeros that tore him apart with cannon-shells as he tried to crawl away. The other three Kittyhawks got airborne but two were shot down, the pilots escaping by parachute, and the third was damaged beyond repair.

Port Darwin's capacious harbour, as Fuchida noted with satisfaction, 'was crowded with all kinds of ships.' In February 1942, even nature conspired to increase the problems of Britain and the Commonwealth countries: on the 2nd, a cyclone had caused so much damage that the harbour could not operate at all until the 10th and not very efficiently thereafter. It had just one wharf, capable of unloading only two ships at a time, their cargoes having to be lifted by cranes onto railway trucks since road transport had no access to the wharf. Water and fuel pipes ran along the wharf, so if ships needed to use these, unloading had to be interrupted. At best it proceeded slowly as a result of difficulties caused partly by Port Darwin's high tidal rise and fall and partly by a poorly-paid, unhappy and unco-operative labour force. In an attempt to speed up the process, ships in the harbour transferred their cargoes into lighters or other small vessels that carried them to hastily-prepared landing sites on the beach. Even so, by 19 February some vessels had waited for almost a fortnight and still not been fully unloaded.

Hence the large number of targets presented to Fuchida's warriors. There was the old American destroyer *Peary* that had come to Port Darwin to refuel after a long but unsuccessful hunt for an enemy submarine. There was the USS *William B. Preston*, also originally designed as a destroyer but now converted into a seaplane tender. There were the vessels of the Royal Australian Navy: the corvettes *Deloraine* and *Katoomba* (the latter under repair in the floating dock), the sloops *Swan* and *Warrego*, the minesweepers *Gunbar*, *Tolga* and *Terka*, the depot ship *Platypus* and numerous smaller craft.

If these made up only a minute fraction of the number of warships that had been at Pearl Harbor, plenty of merchantmen were available as ample compensation. The four troopships that had made the abortive attempt to carry reinforcements to Timor – the American *Meigs*, *Mauna Loa* and *Port Mar* and the Australian *Talagi* – had, mercifully, put their soldiers ashore but were still present themselves. So were the American freighter *Admiral Halstead* and the Australian *Zealandia*, *Neptuna* and *Barossa*, these last two being moored at the wharf. The tankers *British Motorist* – she was indeed British – and *Benjamin Franklin* – perhaps surprisingly she was Norwegian – had arrived with fuel for Port Darwin's oil tanks. Lastly there was the Australian hospital ship *Manunda* that had been intended to go to Singapore but, as a result of earlier developments, had been sent to Port Darwin instead, there to await further orders.

Her presence was soon seen to be providential as Zero fighters, closely followed by Kate high-level bombers, roared in from the landward side. Some of the first bombs dropped hit the wharf. They smashed a huge hole in it, blasted a railway engine bodily into the sea and broke the water pipes and fuel lines. The released fuel ignited, and flames and smoke spread across the wharf and into and over the water.

In the harbour, most of the warships were either already under way or at least had steam up. They made for the open sea, but not quickly enough to save themselves from harm. The Zeros strafed and damaged minesweeper *Gunbar*. HMAS *Swan*, moored at the wharf outboard of the freighter *Neptuna*, hastily cast off but a near miss, exploding close alongside, killed three members of her crew and injured twenty-two more. Depot ship *Platypus* was damaged by near misses, and seaplane tender *William B. Preston* was struck near her stern by a bomb that started a fire but luckily did not halt her.

US destroyer *Peary* proved less fortunate. Fuchida's Kates attacked her with astonishing accuracy. The first bomb to hit her found its mark near her stern and not only wrecked her steering gear but reduced her speed. A second hit started a huge fire that spread rapidly. *Peary* was already blazing furiously, down at the stern and with members of her crew jumping overboard – though her gunners never ceased firing – when three more bombs struck her in quick succession. One of them entered her magazine and she exploded and sank almost immediately. Lieutenant Commander Bermingham, three other officers and seventy-six men were lost.

Hard on the heels of the Kates came the Val dive-bombers. They inflicted further damage on the *William B. Preston*, though not enough to prevent her making good her escape, but in the main they joined with the high-level bombers in assaulting the valuable merchantmen. The largest vessel present, the *Meigs*, received special attention. It has been stated that she took at least twenty bomb hits. She certainly took a large number, burst into flames and sank. Her fellow former troopship *Mauna Loa* was hit by only two bombs but these set her on fire and broke her back; she sank as well. So did the Australian freighter *Zealandia*, also set on fire by two bomb hits, and a couple of small harbour craft. The merchantmen *Port Mar*, *Talagi* and *Admiral Halstead* and the tanker *Benjamin Franklin* were all damaged by near misses and the first two were compelled to beach.

Of course the only British vessel present, the tanker *British*

Motorist, did not escape. A bomb struck her bridge, killing the master, Captain Bates, and starting a fire that was increased by a second hit near the bow that spread her blazing oil across the surface of the harbour where it threatened her crew as they leaped overboard. Minesweeper *Tolga* quickly came to the rescue, pulling them from the sea at some risk to herself, but nothing could save *British Motorist*. She was already listing to port and her list increased until she capsized and sank.

The two ships at the wharf, *Neptuna* and *Barossa*, were both hit in the initial assault and the former was now struck a second time by a bomb that exploded in her boiler room and engulfed her in flames. This was particularly serious since she was loaded with high explosives and depth-charges. There was no way her crew could escape over the wharf which had been shattered by an earlier hit as already recorded and the sea was covered with burning oil from the severed fuel lines. Many men risked going overboard anyway, but *Neptuna* had a large Chinese contingent who were non-swimmers. They remained on her until her lethal cargo blew up in a colossal explosion that sent smoke and flames 300 feet into the air, shook the whole of Port Darwin and hurled fragments of wreckage over neighbouring ships and most of the harbour. Forty-five men lost their lives; more than from any other ship except *Peary*.

One of the vessels rocked by the great explosion was the neighbouring *Barossa*. Her cargo of timber, intended for strengthening Port Darwin's wharf, caught fire. Minesweeper *Tolga* now came to her aid, towing her away from the wharf, but she had to be beached and her fires allowed to burn themselves out. She was later successfully salvaged and towed to safety.[6]

After the Pearl Harbor attack, Commander Fuchida had been asked by Emperor Hirohito for an assurance that no hospital ship had been attacked. This he was able to give and he could have given a similar assurance about the raid on Port Darwin so far as his own high-level Kates were concerned, for they made no attempt to bomb the *Manunda* with her prominent red crosses on decks and funnels. The Val dive-bombers, though, had no such inhibitions. Either because they did not see her markings, as they later stated, or because in their excitement and blood-lust the second-largest ship in the harbour proved an irresistible temptation, they did assault her. One bomb hit and one very near miss caused damage and casualties, but she was still able to evacuate 266 wounded men, of whom, sadly, nineteen died later.

These casualties came not only from ships in the harbour, but also and indeed mainly from ashore. The town of Port Darwin had also been devastated. Shops, houses, offices, the police barracks and the Post Office were destroyed; oil storage tanks were set on fire; and many other buildings were damaged including Government House and the hospital, the latter again by the dive-bombers. The army camp near the town was also hit and Zeros strafed the RAAF station, killing Wing Commander Archibald Tindall who was gallantly firing a machine gun in its defence.

By 1040 the raid was over and Fuchida's men were heading back to their carriers, but their achievements had not yet been completed. Dive-bombers were now sent out to attack the two merchantmen sighted earlier that were hoping to get to the Philippines. The *Florence D* was hit twice and sunk and the *Don Isidro* was hit five times, set on fire and forced to beach, ultimately becoming a total loss. Many of their crews survived, however, as did all except one of the Catalina crew rescued earlier by *Florence D*.

Fuchida had lost only two Vals in the course of the attack, though a Kate and a Zero also failed to return to their carriers. The fighter crash-landed on Melville Island and its pilot, Petty Officer Hajime Toyoshima, was taken prisoner by the local aborigines. His story is a strange one. Richard Connaughton in *Shrouded Secrets: Japan's War on Mainland Australia 1942–44* reports that his subsequent interrogators 'formed an opinion that his heart had not been in the attack and his crash-landing had, therefore, not been accidental.'

Toyoshima told his captors that his name was Tadao Minami. Japanese prisoners often gave false names so that the disgrace of their capture should not be known at home, but Toyoshima went much further. For some reason he declared that he was not a member of the Japanese Navy Air Force but of the Army Air Force; that he was not a pilot but an air-gunner in a bomber; and that his rank was not petty officer but sergeant. On 5 August 1944, he was one of the main instigators of a mass break-out by 344 Japanese prisoners from a camp near the small town of Cowra in New South Wales. This was frankly suicidal in character and 234 of the escapers were indeed killed and the rest recaptured, all except five of them wounded. Toyoshima/Minami was among the dead.[7]

Port Darwin's ordeal was not yet over. Shortly before 1200, twenty-seven Betty bombers from Amboina led by Lieutenant Commander Toshie Irisa and a further twenty-seven from Kendari airfield in Celebes under Lieutenant Commander Takeo Ozaki combined to make a precision strike on the RAAF aerodrome just outside the town. In twenty-five minutes, they effectively destroyed this, demolishing the hangars, equipment stores, administration buildings and sleeping quarters, cratering the runways and wrecking a number of aircraft on the ground, including six Hudsons and Lieutenant Oestreicher's Kittyhawk.

Deplorable consequences followed. Wing Commander Sturt Griffith, the station commander, decided it would be best to withdraw his airmen to a safe rendezvous south of the airfield in case another attack came in. It has been suggested that he should have assembled them all to inform them of his decision but no doubt he wanted to save time that might prove important, so in fact he let his orders be passed from man to man. With the atmosphere that was prevailing, it was perhaps natural that in the process his intentions should come to sound ever more urgent and alarming, and the result was a hurried and disorderly scramble southward that in many cases did not stop at the designated rendezvous point.

The sight of this exodus had the worst possible effect on the civilian population, already shaken by the air-raids and fearing that these were but the prelude to an invasion. Most of them, says Richard Connaughton, 'literally stopped what they were doing and fled.' Some army personnel joined them but the majority took advantage of all the property that had been abandoned and engaged in 'an orgy of drunkenness and looting that lasted for weeks.' The Chinese population had left en masse and the historic Chinese quarter 'was systematically looted and burnt down until all that remained of the old site was a smoking ruin.'

Prime Minister Curtin's immediate reaction to this shocking affair was to pretend it had never happened. In a dramatic speech he announced that: 'In this first battle on Australian soil, it will be a source of pride to the public to know that the armed forces and the civilians comported themselves with the gallantry that is traditional in the people of our stock.' His next reaction was a desperate determination to get hold of the disciplined and battle-hardened Australian troops from the Middle East. If they were not to keep the enemy at a distance by defending the Dutch East Indies, then they must be ready to defend Australia in Australia. Unfortunately, Churchill's fertile mind had suggested another use for some of them and thereby reduced the relationship between the two prime ministers to its lowest ebb.

Whatever may have been stated later, Churchill never wished to prevent Australian troops from defending their homeland and was never unconcerned about the prospect of Australia falling under Japanese domination, but he did believe that the Japanese would never invade Australia. No doubt it was easier to reach this conclusion in London than it was in Canberra, but Churchill's belief was not only reasonable – it was shared by both his firmest ally, President Roosevelt, and his greatest enemy, Adolf Hitler – it was right. The Imperial Navy did consider assaults on Australia (and Hawaii and Ceylon) but the Japanese army chiefs, with Japan's new conquests to guard and her endless war in China to fight, never for a moment considered providing the troops that would be necessary and all these projects were abandoned as impracticable.

On the other hand, Churchill accepted that it was only natural that the Australian government should fear that a Japanese invasion might be imminent. It does therefore appear that, regardless of the strategic advantages of his latest plan, this was so unwise diplomatically that it would have been better had it never been mentioned. Of course Churchill, shaken by the ruin of all his hopes in North Africa, the Channel Dash, the fall of Singapore and the whole endless sequence of lesser misfortunes, was by now becoming desperate for some compensating success.

What probably triggered Churchill's action was Wavell's signal of 16 February. While advising against reinforcing Java, this had stated that 'Burma and Australia are absolutely vital for war against Japan.' Churchill may have been sure that Australia was not in danger of invasion, but Burma had already been invaded and matters were going badly there. It will be remembered that Churchill had earlier considered diverting forces intended for Singapore to Burma and he now turned to a similar scheme.

Wavell's signal had added that: 'Immediate problem is destination of Australian Corps.' The bulk of 7th Australian Division was then being shipped over the Indian Ocean and Churchill, as he signalled to Curtin on 20 February, wished it to be directed to Burma where it could arrive on about the 27th and perhaps prevent the loss of the Burmese capital, Rangoon. Churchill pleaded that 7th Australian was the only force in the world that was available and confirmed that 6th Australian Division would not be so diverted. Roosevelt, on Churchill's prompting, added his request to that of Britain's prime minister.

Curtin, with the bombing of Port Darwin fresh in his mind, flatly refused. He protested at Churchill sending 'a rather strongly worded request at this late date', harped once more on past British failures and past Australian services and indicated with insulting directness that he doubted Churchill's assurances that if 7th Australian Division went to Burma the rest of I Australian Corps would not be asked to follow it.

This message was sent on 22 February. Unhappily, Churchill had been certain that the Australians would not fail him, particularly since his pleas had been echoed by the US president, to whose country, according to Curtin, Australia now looked. On the previous day, therefore, with no reply received, he had diverted the troopships on his own responsibility in order to avoid delay. He was now compelled, presumably with some embarrassment, to admit this and most unwisely took the opportunity to suggest that Curtin might care to reconsider. The Australian government, understandably incensed that Churchill appeared to have 'treated our approval to this vital diversion as merely a matter of form', stated flatly that it was 'quite impossible to reverse a decision which we made with the utmost care, and which we have affirmed and reaffirmed.' Churchill had no choice but to comply.

The lack of trust and confidence in him shown by the Australians, whom he genuinely admired, wounded Churchill deeply and added to the strain and depression from which he appears to have been suffering at the time. Ironically it had all been pointless for if 7th Australian Division had gone to Rangoon as Churchill wished, it seems certain that it would have been unable to prevent the loss of the city, which in practice meant the loss of the whole colony. The telegram containing the final Australian refusal was dated 23 February. On the same day in Burma, utter catastrophe befell the British forces and the British cause at the bridge on the Sittang River.

Notes

1. In July 1940, Japanese pressure forced Britain to close the Burma Road but it was reopened in October.

2. It is often stated that the presence of *Indomitable* might have saved *Prince of Wales* and *Repulse* from destruction. In fact, Japan's airmen were so able that the handful of Fleet Air Arm fighters on board her would have been unlikely to have done more than make them pay more heavily for their success. Indeed, they might well have added to that success by sinking *Indomitable* as well.

3. By contrast, Churchill would more than once acknowledge his indebtedness to Curtin for allowing the third Australian division, Morshead's 9th Australian, to remain in the Middle East, where it would later play a vital part in Eighth Army's great victory at El Alamein.

4. The Portuguese authorities were much displeased by the presence of the Australians; believing, rightly, that it would provoke an attack on them that the Japanese had not otherwise intended and the Australians would not be strong enough to prevent.

5. It was the warships guarding this convoy that sank or captured the vessels fleeing from Singapore, as already described.

6. An ironical footnote, this one. Many years later, the wrecks of the vessels that had been sunk at Port Darwin were also salvaged and towed away for scrap, by a firm with a name very similar to that of the leader of the raid responsible for their sinking, the Fujita Company of Osaka.

7. Richard Connaughton's *Shrouded Secrets* gives a detailed account of the Cowra drama and of the part played in it by Toyoshima/Minami.

Chapter 7

The Bridge on the
Sittang River

Churchill's failure to anticipate Australian reaction to his diversion of the troop convoy was only one of those erroneous assumptions that provide an ironical background to events in Burma in February 1942. As we have seen, Wavell considered that the retention of Burma was 'absolutely vital' for a successful prosecution of the war against Japan. Churchill feared that its loss and the consequent severance of the Burma Road would be followed by the collapse of Chinese resistance and a Japanese invasion of India. Both were completely, if mercifully, wrong.

The disasters that befell the British in February 1942 guaranteed the Japanese capture of Rangoon. This is turn deprived the British of the port to which their reinforcements were sent and enabled their enemies to use it for the same purpose. They promptly exploited their advantage and by early May, the whole of Burma was in their hands. Not until early May 1945 did the British re-enter Rangoon, but in the three years that had elapsed, the war against Japan had been so little handicapped that it was on the verge of a triumphant conclusion.

In the previous October, the Imperial Japanese Navy had lost so heavily in the gigantic Battle of Leyte Gulf that it was no longer a factor to be reckoned with. The Americans had followed up their victory by regaining the Philippines and this, coupled with the destruction of Japan's merchant marine by US submarines, had by May 1945 effectively severed Japan's supply lines to those conquests in the south for which she had gone to war in the first place. In the air, American bombers, practically unopposed, were delivering increasingly destructive raids on Japanese cities, with which the civil authorities were quite unable to cope. On land, the American Tenth Army was proceeding steadily, though slowly and at great cost, with the conquest of the island of Okinawa, the last stop before the invasion of the Japanese homeland. The ownership of Rangoon was a matter of minimal importance.

There was, however, the consolation that the original British loss of Burma had not had the dire consequences that Churchill and Wavell had feared. Not only did Burma prove not to be vital for carrying on the war against Japan, but the severing of the Burma Road did not bring an end to Chinese resistance. Moreover, although for propaganda purposes both sides would later refer to a 'March on Delhi', in reality the Japanese never had any intention of invading India, which was linked with Burma only by a few inadequate tracks passing through appalling natural obstacles.

In fact Burma was, for the Japanese, a secondary theatre of operations and their occupation of it was at bottom a defensive measure, designed to establish a bulwark, blocking any British counter-offensive from the north against Malaya and the East Indies. They therefore saw no point in mounting a full-scale invasion of Burma until reasonable progress had been made in these more valuable areas. Throughout the whole of December 1941, the only move the Japanese made into Burma was their occupation of the airfield at Victoria Point in the extreme south of the colony, and this so that British fighter aircraft could not be flown from it to reinforce Malaya.

Japan's Army Air Force was more active. On 23 December a raid on Rangoon killed or wounded over 2,000 civilians who, being quite unused to aerial warfare, had poured onto the streets to watch the bombers rather than seeking shelter from them. A larger raid on Christmas Day caused only about 100 casualties, but this was mainly because, by that time, most of its inhabitants had fled the city. The Burmese took shelter in local villages but about 100,000 Indians made for the northern frontier, spreading panic among the communities through which they passed. This flight resulted in a breakdown of Rangoon's essential services. Even the dock labourers had left and troops arriving later had to unload their own equipment.

Then on 15 January 1942, Japanese forces from Thailand invaded Tenasserim, the 500-mile-long 'tail' of Burma running down the western side of the Kra Isthmus. Their main objectives were the airfields at Moulmein, Tavoy and Mergui, reading from north to south, from which RAF aircraft had been raiding Japanese bases in Thailand. Tavoy fell on the 19th and this cut off the garrison at Mergui which was evacuated by sea next day. Moulmein on the east bank of the mouth of the Salween River was captured on the morning of the 31st. Its defenders were carried in river steamers to Martaban on the west bank of the Salween which now marked the front line.

These gains had been achieved by Japan's Fifteenth Army under Lieutenant General Shojiro Iida. The title of his command was more impressive than real for at this stage it consisted of only one division, the 55th Infantry under Lieutenant General Yutaka Takeuchi, and this controlled just two regiments, each only two battalions strong. On 6 February, however, Lieutenant General Shozo Sakurai's 33rd Infantry Division also moved into Burma from Thailand and made for Pa-an, some 20 miles upstream from Moulmein on the eastern bank of the Salween. Sakurai also commanded only two regiments but both were at their full strength of three battalions, the men of which had earned a deserved reputation in the fighting in China and were trained, experienced and battle-hardened.

Burma's defenders could not match the Japanese soldiers in quality but, as in Malaya and Singapore, they were superior in numbers. At one time it appeared that they would be greatly superior, for Chiang Kai-shek, worried about the safety of his supply lines, had offered to send large Chinese contingents to Burma's aid. General Wavell, however, although ultimately responsible for Burma's protection as either Commander-in-Chief, India or Supreme Commander of ABDA, refused to accept them, and so curtly that he caused needless offence.

Wavell's decision has aroused understandable criticism but the fact was that Chinese troops, as H.P. Willmott puts it in his *Empires in the Balance*, 'had a reputation for acquisitiveness that placed them second only to locusts.' They were invariably short of supplies and therefore lived off the land; when they did enter Burma later, according to Major General James Lunt in *A Hell of a Licking: The Retreat from Burma 1941–2*, 'they travelled the country like the Tartar hordes, looting, stealing and burning.' This did nothing to encourage Burmese loyalty to the Allied cause. Moreover, as Wavell was well aware, China laid claim to Upper Burma and while Burma's inhabitants did not much like British rule, they vastly preferred it to a possible Chinese takeover.

To command the Burma Army, Wavell appointed his own chief of staff in India, Lieutenant General Thomas Hutton, whom he knew would loyally follow his (Wavell's) requirements. Hutton was a man of undoubted personal courage and a brilliant and far-sighted staff officer. He can claim a great deal of the credit for saving the Burma Army from total destruction because, in order that it might survive even if Rangoon was lost, he ordered his chief administrative officer, Major General Goddard, to transfer three-quarters of all reserve stocks of food and petrol to depots in the vicinity of Mandalay. Despite all difficulties, the move was completed by early March 1942, just in time.

Unfortunately, since the First World War Hutton had served only on staff appointments, he knew little of the troops under his command, and he was not a strong or forceful personality. Major General Lunt states that when he first met Hutton in early February 1942, he noted in his diary that his superior looked 'more like a head gardener than a general'.

Nor was Hutton's conduct of the Burma campaign in February 1942 helped by the fact that he was not fully fit. As the situation worsened, the British decided to accept the offer of Chinese help after all and on the night of 2/3 February, Hutton and his ADC, Lieutenant Nigel Chancellor, set out for Lashio in northern Burma in a pair of Lysander aircraft to finalize the arrangements with Chiang. Flying in total darkness, the Lysanders lost their way and Hutton's pilot, Flight Lieutenant Tate, attempted to land in a jungle clearing. The aircraft crashed, knocking out the pilot and trapping him in his cockpit; it then caught fire. Hutton, though badly bruised, was able to get clear. For a ghastly half-hour he kept the flames under control by beating them with his uniform jacket, until a party of villagers came to his aid and pulled out Tate who, sadly, died a few days later.

Meanwhile, the pilot of the second Lysander, Flight Lieutenant Mann, found that his landing lights were not working and suggested that Chancellor had best parachute to the clearing. Though he had never used a parachute and indeed only once before been in an aircraft, Chancellor did so, ending up in a tree with minor injuries. Mann then tried to land his machine, but also crashed. He proved luckier than Tate but his Lysander was a total loss. Hutton and his ADC proceeded by rail to Lashio, where there was just time to complete arrangements with Chiang before Hutton had to hurry to Rangoon to meet Wavell who had flown in from Java.

One reason for the decision to accept Chiang's offer was that a number of intended reinforcements for Burma – 18th (British) Division, for example – had been sent to Malaya or Singapore instead. In addition, Major General Bruce Scott's 1st Burma Division containing 1st Burma Brigade and 13th Indian Brigade had had to be stationed in the vicinity of Mandalay since Allied Intelligence considered that the Japanese might make a secondary thrust here from northern Thailand.

That left the task of resisting Iida's Fifteenth Army to 17th Indian Division commanded by Brigadier (acting Major General) John 'Jackie' Smyth VC. Of his original three brigades, two had gone to fight and be destroyed in Malaya and Singapore, only 46th Indian Brigade remaining under his command. Prior to February 1942, though, this had been joined by 2nd Burma Brigade, 16th Indian Brigade and 48th Brigade of Gurkhas.

In theory, Smyth also had the support of the RAF units in Burma – two squadrons of Hurricanes, one of Buffaloes, one of Blenheim bombers and two of Lysanders[1] – supplemented by the Tomahawks of Colonel Claire Chennault's American Volunteer Group, the famous 'Flying Tigers' that had previously fought for Chiang Kai-shek. Yet in practice, the fighters at least were chiefly engaged in opposing the Sally bombers and their Nate or Oscar fighter escorts that were attacking Rangoon. They inflicted considerable damage on these, but the Japanese could replace their losses and the British and Americans could not.

This was by no means the only respect in which the British position on the Salween was weaker than it might appear. Of 17th Indian Division's four brigades, both 2nd Burma and 16th Indian contained a high proportion of inexperienced recruits and had been shaken by earlier clashes with the Japanese in which they had suffered heavy losses of men, equipment and transport. Since 48th Gurkha Brigade was held back as a reserve until Japanese intentions became clear, the Salween was in fact defended only by Brigadier Roger Ekin's 46th Indian Brigade, reinforced by the 2nd Battalion KOYLI (King's Own Yorkshire Light Infantry).

Moreover, Smyth was even less well than Hutton. In the previous October, he had had a serious operation and the problem had now resurfaced. Smyth always remained outwardly cheerful and a medical board set up under 17th Division's chief doctor, Colonel Mackenzie, found him fit enough to remain at his post. This, though, was probably at Smyth's insistence for the board also recommended that he be granted two months' sick leave as soon as the military situation had stabilized. In reality, Smyth's every movement was painful, he could only keep going with the aid of strychnine injections and Brigadier Ekin for one was convinced that he was a very sick man whose condition was responsible for some of the strange decisions that he would make.

To add to the strain on Smyth, he had been much concerned by having received orders that were quite contrary to his own beliefs and wishes. There were three southward-flowing rivers that could provide potential obstacles between Iida's Fifteenth Army and its objective, Rangoon, itself standing on the eastern branch of the Irrawaddy River Delta. The most easterly was the Salween. This was 7,000 yards wide at its mouth between Moulmein and Martaban, but upstream it flowed through hills covered by dense jungle that would mask the approach of the Japanese but not hinder them and where there were local ferries that they could use. It would be difficult to defend without a much larger force than the one Smyth had available. Some 50 miles west of the Salween was the much smaller Bilin River. This was crossed by only one good bridge but, except in the monsoon season, it was possible to wade over it quite easily.

Smyth therefore wished to fight only delaying actions at the Salween and Bilin and make his main stand a further 50 miles or so to the west at the Sittang River. This was a much more formidable obstacle, up to 600 yards wide and with a fast-flowing current that made it very difficult to cross. It was spanned by just a single – and single-tracked – railway bridge. Furthermore, there was open country on its west bank that Smyth believed would well suit 16th and 46th brigades, trained for combat in North Africa, and would allow the excellent British artillery to be most effective.

His superiors had different ideas. Wavell, astonishingly, still did not regard the Japanese as worthy enemies. He wished to hold as far forward as possible, feared that constant retreats would damage the morale of the troops and believed that adopting a bold policy would be more effective and less expensive. As late as 21 February, he would demand that: 'You must stop all further withdrawal and counter-attack whenever possible.'

Wavell's attitude was fully supported by Burma's governor, Sir Reginald Dorman-Smith, who naturally wished to preserve the integrity of his colony. Moreover the mouth of the Sittang is only 100 miles north-east of Rangoon, and the Gulf of Martaban into which it flows bites so deeply into the south coast of Burma that should the Japanese cross the river, an advance due westward would automatically sever the line of retreat from the capital. Dorman-Smith feared that if the Japanese came so close to Rangoon, the threat of this happening would destroy what was left of the city's morale.

Lieutenant General Hutton was more pessimistic, or perhaps one should say more realistic, but he too considered that Smyth should fight as far forward as possible. This was partly because he loyally did his best to meet his chief's wishes and partly because it was his personal belief that the enemy should be kept well away from Rangoon. British reinforcements had to come to Rangoon and Hutton wisely wanted them to be given plenty of time to acclimatize to the local conditions before being sent into action.

All British wishes and intentions were, however, swept away by the Japanese taking the initiative. While heavy air-raids put pressure on the defenders, Japan's 55th Infantry Division crossed the Salween north of Martaban on 9 February. This cut off Martaban's garrison, 3/7th Gurkhas and a company of 2nd KOYLI, and although these drove back the first attacks, it was clear that they would not be able to hold out for long. Orders were therefore sent that they should withdraw, but these were never received: the British wireless sets at this time were not reliable and a liaison officer, Second Lieutenant Jolly, bringing verbal confirmation was killed in a Japanese ambush. Happily, the garrison commander, Lieutenant Colonel Stevenson, had already decided that his position was untenable. Having destroyed his motor transport, he broke out of the trap, his exhausted troops reaching Thaton, 50 miles to the north, on 11 February.

Also on the 11th, Japan's 33rd Infantry Division crossed the Salween some 2 miles south of the town of Kuzeik, due east of Thaton. At 0045 on the 12th, Kuzeik's defenders, the 7/10th Baluchis, came under attack from Japanese forces that quickly built up to an entire regiment in strength. Despite the odds against them, the Baluchis resisted magnificently until 0900, when they were finally compelled to retreat. Their CO, Lieutenant Colonel Dyer, was killed and only 5 officers, 3 Viceroy's Commissioned Officers and 65 men were able to escape to Thaton.[2]

By the afternoon of 13 February, 33rd Infantry Division had advanced to Duyinzeik, north-east of Thaton, and here it subjected the garrison, 5/17th Dogras, to a forty-five-minute artillery and mortar bombardment. Surprisingly, this was not followed by an infantry attack but Smyth, fearing that Duyinzeik could not long resist and its capture would enable the enemy to cut off his troops in Thaton, decided he must abandon both places. At 1740 on the 14th, he moved all his men back to the Bilin River.

Smyth would have preferred to have moved them right back to the Sittang, but he had rashly announced that 17th Indian Division could put up a good fight in the Bilin area and thereby ended any faint chance of obtaining Hutton's approval. Certainly 17th Indian was stronger now. The battered 2nd Burma Brigade had been sent to guard the lines of communication in the Sittang valley on 12 February, and would be transferred to 1st Burma Division on the 28th, but 16th Indian Brigade had been rested and reinforced and the Gurkhas of 48th Brigade had moved up to the front line. Smyth detailed these two formations to hold the Bilin while the larger part of 46th Indian Brigade formed his reserve, stationed at Kyaikto, halfway between the Bilin and the Sittang.

Once again, British hopes were dashed by Japanese speed of movement. Lieutenant General Sakurai's 33rd Infantry Division followed up Smyth's retreat so rapidly that on 16 February its 214th Regiment broke across the Bilin near the town of Ahonwa on 17th Indian Division's left flank before the area's defenders, 16th Indian Brigade, could take up its defensive positions. For the rest of that day and most of the following one, 16th Indian tried to drive the Japanese back but without success.

Smyth therefore felt he had no option but to send troops from 48th Brigade to 16th Indian's assistance. At 1730 on the 17th, the 1st Battalion of the 4th Gurkha Rifles, supported by artillery, recaptured the strategically important village of Danyingon and a neighbouring jungle-covered hill called Point 313, an achievement recognized by the award of a DSO to the Gurkhas' CO, Lieutenant Colonel Lentaigne. Yet the Japanese still held on to their bridgehead across the Bilin and on 18 February made a determined attempt to regain Danyingon that was only checked by artillery fire and strikes by the RAF.

Meanwhile, 17th Indian Division had come under attack elsewhere. It is a tribute to the way in which the Japanese could move so much more rapidly than their British and Commonwealth opponents that on 17 February they caught one of Smyth's battalions, 5/17th Dogras, still in the town of Bilin on the river's eastern bank. Attacked by Sakurai's other regiment, the 215th, by 1530 it had been driven back over the Bilin with the loss of most of its weapons. That night, the 215th Regiment crossed the river in pursuit and assaulted Smyth's centre. Though 8th Burma Rifles offered staunch resistance, the Japanese pushed forward slowly but steadily and were only checked on the 18th by a counter-attack delivered by 2/5th Gurkhas.

To complete the pressure on Smyth, also on 18 February units of Japan's 55th Infantry Division mounted an amphibious operation that came ashore, virtually without resistance, at Zokali some 5 miles west of the Bilin, threatening Smyth's right flank and rear as well as his line of retreat. That afternoon, Smyth advised Hutton that 16th Brigade had been 'fought to a standstill', that he had brought 46 Brigade's 4/12th Frontier Force Regiment forward from Kyaikto to stiffen the resistance on his left flank but this was his last battalion 'really capable of active operations', and that he now had this new enemy force 'approaching along the coast' to deal with as well.

The position of 17th Indian Division had in fact become impossible, as was recognized by Hutton when he came to see the situation for himself on 19 February. He therefore gave his approval for Smyth to withdraw behind the Sittang as soon as he could break off the action at the Bilin, which would be difficult during the hours of daylight.

Although the stand on the Bilin has been subjected to much critical comment, it can be credited with several useful achievements. It had at last checked the momentum of the Japanese who had incurred heavy casualties and were somewhat shaken by the most fierce and determined resistance they had yet encountered in Burma. It had also gained time for reinforcements to reach Rangoon by sea. The 2nd Battalion, Duke of Wellington's Regiment (the Dukes) had already arrived on 14 February, though without its transport vehicles that were following in a later convoy. On the 21st, the 1st Cameronians landed and on the same day, so did Brigadier John Anstice's 7th Armoured Brigade. This consisted of the 7th Queen's Own Hussars, the 2nd Battalion of the Royal Tank Regiment, the 414th Battery, Royal Artillery and the 95th Anti-Tank Regiment, and its presence would prove invaluable in the later Burma campaigns.

These advantages did not appease Wavell, who from faraway Java still believed that a resolute commander and bolder tactics would easily save the situation. Wavell had been enraged by 17th Indian Division's retreat to the Bilin and his wrath was in no way abated by a gloomy, if entirely accurate situation report from Hutton on 18 February. In this, Hutton made it clear that it seemed certain 17th

Indian would have to fall back behind the Sittang and unless it made a successful stand there, Rangoon could not be held. Wavell responded with a series of angry signals demanding a counter-offensive, preferably one made east of the Sittang.

Hutton had issued the same warning to the governor, Dorman-Smith, who was greatly alarmed and two days later took the first steps in a plan for evacuating civilians from Rangoon. Hutton followed this up on 21 February by instructing administrative units that had been among the arrivals at Rangoon on this date to return at once to India. It seems that this finally ended Wavell's confidence in him. On the 22nd, with the feeble excuse that the strength of the Burma Army was increasing rapidly, Hutton was told he would be replaced as its head by Lieutenant General Sir Harold Alexander as soon as that officer could be sent out from Britain.

It appears that Wavell, and to a lesser extent Hutton, had lost confidence in Smyth as well and certainly Smyth would give them cause for this during the retreat to and fighting at the Sittang. It may seem brutally unfeeling to criticize an officer who was not only confronted by immense difficulties and a capable, determined and ruthless enemy but was mentally exhausted and physically in constant and considerable pain; nonetheless, some of his decisions are very difficult to justify or even explain.

Smyth's first duty was to break contact with the enemy and this he did successfully. The 16th Brigade, exhausted and badly mauled, fell back first in the early hours of 20 February, covered by 48th Brigade. The Gurkhas could only follow after RAF bombers had delivered a heavy raid on the Japanese, though sadly this inflicted some casualties on them as well, so closely were the two sides engaged. Shortly after noon, both 16th and 48th brigades were retiring safely towards Kyaikto where the bulk of 46th Brigade was already stationed.

Then, however, matters started to go wrong. Smyth's next task was to bring his division not just to but behind the Sittang. There were some ferries and small craft that could be used to get the soldiers across the river, but the main way over was that single railway bridge, now covered with planks so that it could take motor vehicles. It was an impressive structure with eleven spans, each 150 feet long, though its appearance had been marred by its steel having rusted to a colour that some felt looked ominously like that of dried blood.

It was obviously essential that the bridge should not fall into the hands of the Japanese, but on 20 February the force guarding it consisted of little more than 3rd Burma Rifles, detached from 2nd Burma Brigade and only 200 strong. Hutton had sent the 2nd Dukes to the bridge on the previous day, but Smyth had ordered the main part of the battalion forward to Kyaikto where it arrived on the 20th; an inexplicable action since he knew it would shortly be falling back to the bridge with the rest of 17th Division in any case. Only one company remained at the bridge and this on the far or western bank, though with orders to counter-attack over it if necessary. In addition, 7/10th Baluchis guarded supply dumps at the village of Mokpalin just south-east of the bridge, but this battalion too was very low in numbers after the battering it had received at Kuzeik on 12 February.

Brigadier Ekin, whose 46th Indian Brigade was closest to the Sittang, was convinced that the defenders of the bridge were far too few in numbers and was concerned that the Japanese, as on several previous occasions, would attempt to bypass the British and Commonwealth soldiers, speed directly to the river and so cut off Smyth's retreat. He suggested that his brigade and all vehicles not immediately required should leave at once for the bridge, thereby both strengthening its garrison and speeding up 17th Division's withdrawal to and over it. Unhappily, Smyth insisted that 46th Brigade remain at Kyaikto, providing a firm base, until both his other brigades had passed through it, and only then follow them, acting as the rearguard with the aid of the luckless 2nd Dukes.

It was a fatal mistake, for Ekin's fears of Japanese outflanking movements were well-founded and it was made worse by an earlier error. On the night of 19/20 February, one at least of 17th Indian's formations had broadcast its orders for retirement in plain English. The 33rd Infantry Division's Signals Unit intercepted the message and Lieutenant General Sakurai promptly instructed his 215th Regiment to make for the bridge through the jungle north of Kyaikto, while part of his 214th Regiment followed hard on the heels of 17th Indian and the rest moved south of Smyth's line of retreat in the hope of cutting him off from this direction also.

To make matters worse, 17th Indian was not aware of the extent of its danger. For some time, indeed, it appeared that it would make its escape reasonably easily. A good road ran from the Bilin as far as Kyaikto, which 16th and 48th brigades had reached by the evening of 20 February, and where they had a chance to recover from their exhaustion. At 0500 next morning, the Japanese made a raid on Smyth's tactical headquarters – he had sent the bulk of his staff on to Mokpalin – but Smyth reports that 'apart from creating some confusion and firing off a lot of ammunition, they achieved little and drew off at daybreak.'

Soon after daybreak the retirement continued, the first troops to leave being 4/12th Frontier Force which, rather ironically, had not long before been part of Ekin's 46th Brigade. It was accompanied by Captain Robert Orgill's Malerkotla Field Company whose task was to prepare the Sittang bridge for demolition once 17th Indian Division had crossed it. The 48th Brigade consisting of 1/3rd, 1/4th and 2/5th Gurkha Rifles and commanded by Brigadier Noel Hugh-Jones followed, but 16th and 46th brigades were not able to set out until the morning of 22 February.

The 'road' from Kyaikto to Mokpalin was a rough track, hemmed in by dense jungle, hardly wide enough to allow two vehicles to pass each other and covered with a thick red dust. On the other hand, it was considerably better than the jungle paths the Japanese had to negotiate in their outflanking moves. Unfortunately, as the British and Commonwealth troops retired along it, they were repeatedly bombed and strafed by both enemy and Allied aircraft, the Flying Tigers' Tomahawks making especially destructive strikes; by a deplorable lack of co-ordination, the British and American airmen had been advised that only hostile forces were to be found east of the Sittang.

These attacks caused casualties and destroyed numerous vehicles. Others, including ambulances full of wounded men, had to be abandoned. Worst of all, the retreat was much delayed. It was not until late in the evening that 4/12th Frontier Force and Orgill's sappers arrived at the bridge, the former to swell the ranks of its defenders and the latter setting to work at once to fit demolition charges on it. At about the same time, 1/4th Gurkhas, the leading formation of 48th Brigade, reached Mokpalin.

That evening also, Smyth came to the bridge, as did Brigadier Hugh-Jones and 48th Brigade Headquarters. At about midnight on 21/22 February, Smyth was warned by a staff officer sent from Rangoon that British Intelligence believed the Japanese might make a parachute landing in the open country on the far side of the Sittang. Both Smyth and Hugh-Jones took their headquarters across the river and Smyth ordered 1/4th Gurkhas over it forthwith and intended that 48th Brigade's other two battalions and 7/10th Baluchis should follow in due course.

Meanwhile, 17th Division's transport had also started to go over the bridge. All went well until 0400 on the 22nd when a lorry ran off the planking to become jammed in the bridge's girders. It was not until 0630 that the obstacle could be removed and by early morning, a great number of vehicles were still on the eastern bank, among them some field ambulances with their medical personnel. Smyth visited them to talk to his senior doctor, Colonel Mackenzie, and was just re-crossing the bridge to his headquarters when, at 0830, a burst of rifle and mortar fire announced that Sakurai's 215th Regiment had caught up with him.

Throughout 21 February, Smyth had received no news of the enemy since the attack on his tactical headquarters in the early hours. In fact, at 1430, 215th Regiment had clashed with a small reconnaissance unit while proceeding on its outflanking movement to the north of Smyth's line of retreat. Yet, astonishingly, no report of this encounter was ever sent to 17th Indian Division's commander.

Consequently, the initial Japanese onslaught on the morning of the 22nd achieved complete surprise. Attacking from the north-east, units from 215th Regiment struck at both the Sittang River bridge and Mokpalin village. Their first assault shattered 3rd Burma Rifles, seized two key positions known as Pagoda and Buddha Hills after the building and statue on their respective summits, destroyed many of the vehicles awaiting their turn to cross the bridge and took numerous prisoners including Colonel Mackenzie. Only a gallant counter-attack by 4/12th Frontier Force prevented them from reaching the bridge and they posed so great a threat that its defenders hastily destroyed three power-driven ferries and some 300 small boats that could otherwise have assisted in carrying the troops over the Sittang, fearing that they might be captured by the enemy.

Fighting in the vicinity of the bridge continued all day but 4/12th Frontier Force, aided by the company of the 2nd Dukes returning to the river's eastern bank and 7/10th Baluchis, arriving from Mokpalin just before the Japanese attacked, offered sturdy resistance. The defenders even managed to retake Pagoda Hill, though at heavy cost. In the afternoon, Japanese reinforcements arrived to increase the pressure, but Smyth sent 1/4th Gurkhas back over the bridge and the Japanese could make no further progress.

They had, however, been able to place a strong body of troops across the road between the bridge and Mokpalin over which the rest of 17th Indian Division would have to retreat. Their initial thrust carried them right into Mokpalin but 48th Brigade's other two battalions had reached it during the previous night and 2/5th Gurkhas checked the attack and then pushed the attackers back. The 1/3rd Gurkhas, though still exhausted from their night march, followed up and captured Buddha Hill in the face of fierce resistance. The Gurkhas' success was marred by the death of their CO, Lieutenant Colonel Ballinger, who was killed by a small enemy group that had pretended to surrender; it had still not been realized that unwounded Japanese soldiers were never likely to allow themselves to be taken prisoner. Then the enemy hit back and the Gurkhas on Buddha Hill were isolated.

While the struggle at the bridge was raging, 17th Division's 16th and 46th brigades, moving down the dusty track towards Mokpalin, were coming under constant flank attacks by Sakurai's 214th Regiment and strikes by the Japanese Army Air Force. The 16th Brigade reached Mokpalin only in the late afternoon; 46th Brigade was trailing a mile behind and at one point the Japanese managed to block the track in front of it. Ekin's men finally forced their way past but in the process became badly dispersed. The main part of the brigade got to Mokpalin at about 1700, but detached parties were still coming in for some time thereafter.

At Mokpalin now were 16th and 46th Indian brigades and 1/3rd and 2/5th Gurkhas from 48th Brigade, but they were quite unable to cover the mile of road still between them and the Sittang River bridge. Indeed, they were hard-pressed to hold their ground, for as darkness fell, 215th Regiment resumed its attacks on the village from the north while 214th Regiment assaulted it from the east and south. Only the British artillery, in constant action and often firing over open sights, kept the Japanese at bay.

Back at the bridge, the fighting had died down at nightfall. Smyth had already transferred his headquarters staff to Abya, some 8 miles to the west, and he now decided to go there himself, accompanied by Brigadier Cowan[3] whom Smyth, with Hutton's consent, had appointed his Brigadier General Staff. Smyth was due to meet Hutton next day and he would thus reduce the distance he would have to travel. Yet Hutton would later criticize Smyth's failure to remain at the bridge and it is perhaps surprising that, having been allowed a Brigadier General Staff, a position not normally found in formations smaller than a corps, Smyth did not send Cowan to confer with Hutton who, incidentally, trusted Cowan completely. This would have permitted Smyth to have remained at the Sittang where a dreadful dilemma would soon have to be solved.

As it was, a fearful responsibility was placed on the shoulders of Brigadier Hugh-Jones, to whom the defence of the bridge was now entrusted. Orgill's sappers had completed their preparations for its destruction by 1800, and Smyth made it clear to Hugh-Jones that whatever happened, the bridge must not be captured intact by the Japanese since this would enable them to march on Rangoon forthwith.

Smyth did wish to have the final word as to when the charges should be detonated unless it proved impossible for Hugh-Jones to get in touch with him. Clearly, though, as the man on the spot, Hugh-Jones would have to recommend the bridge's destruction and as Smyth would not be able to see and assess the situation for himself, it was hardly likely that he would not accept the recommendation. Yet British wireless sets were so poor that, despite desperate efforts to contact them, Hugh-Jones had no idea of the exact whereabouts of 16th and 46th brigades or even of 48th Brigade's own battalions apart from 1/4th Gurkhas. If the bridge was destroyed before they could reach it, all these forces would be trapped between the Japanese and the river.

During the night, the Japanese resumed their attacks on the bridge's defenders, who were becoming exhausted and fast running out of ammunition. It seemed certain that they would be unable to repel a major assault and in any case at about 0200 on 23 February, Hugh-Jones was warned by Orgill that if the bridge was not destroyed during the hours of darkness, it might well be impossible for this to be done, under fire, in daylight.

By 0430, Hugh-Jones felt that he could no longer postpone his agonizing decision. He therefore telephoned Smyth, informed his superior that he could not guarantee to hold the bridge for more than another hour and asked for permission to destroy it. This Smyth gave. Hugh-Jones at once began to bring the bridge's garrison back over it to the western bank. As soon as they had all reached this, the orders were given, Lieutenant Bashir Ahmed Khan pressed the plunger, there was a colossal explosion and two of the bridge's spans fell into the river.

The only reliable means of retreat for the trapped formations of 17th Indian Division had gone. Shortly before dawn on 23 February, 1/3rd Gurkhas on Buddha Hill was finally overrun: only 107 of its men would survive the Battle of the Sittang River. The remaining troops came under constant artillery and mortar fire, while at 1115 a raid by twenty-seven Japanese bombers caused heavy casualties and set a number of vehicles on fire. At 1430, it was decided that the majority of the men should abandon the transport and head for the river, leaving only a covering force to hold back the Japanese. This force continued to resist until 1930, when it too was compelled to retreat to the Sittang.

For all those troops who reached the river, its fast-flowing waters presented a daunting obstacle. Several turned back and were taken prisoner. Others fled into the jungle to search for an easier crossing-place upstream. Most, though, attempted to get to the far bank, either by swimming or paddling rafts or logs. Many succeeded, among them Brigadier Ekin and the commander of 16th Indian Brigade, Brigadier Jones, but a considerable number drowned or were killed by snipers or strafing aircraft. Even those who made the crossing were not safe. Lieutenant Colonel Basil Owen, the popular and respected CO of 2nd Dukes, completely exhausted from his swim, sought food and rest in a Burmese village. The villagers murdered him.

Casualties were horrific, particularly in those battalions, coming mainly from 46th Indian Brigade, that had provided the rearguard: 3/7th Gurkhas was reduced to a strength of 170; 5/17th Dogras to 104; 8th Burma Rifles to 96. The whole of 46th Brigade could muster just 798 men. It was therefore disbanded and its survivors transferred to 48th and 16th brigades; these certainly needed reinforcements since their own numbers were down to 1,516 and 1,170 respectively.

For the time being, 17th Indian Division had ceased to exist as an effective fighting formation. It now numbered just 80 British officers, 69 Indian or Gurkha officers and 3,335 other ranks and was almost without transport, artillery and equipment. Some 6,000 personal weapons had been lost and the division could find only 56 light machine guns, 62 tommy-guns and 1,420 rifles. Most of the men who had swum the river had lost their boots and many had lost the rest of their clothing as well. Disaster had been complete and absolute.

There would be one final, if long-delayed tragedy. Although Smyth always accepted full responsibility for the demolition of the bridge, Brigadier Noel Hugh-Jones could never forget his own part in its destruction and the ghastly consequences that had followed. They preyed upon his mind to such an extent that some years later he committed suicide by drowning himself; the last British casualty of the Battle of the Sittang River.

Fortunately the Japanese soldiers were themselves short of ammunition and on the verge of complete exhaustion, and with good reason. In just over a month, they had advanced nearly 200 miles, mainly by way of rough jungle tracks and without proper supply facilities. Iida was at last compelled to pause while his forces were rested and reorganized. It would be another week before 33rd and 55th Infantry divisions crossed the Sittang.

In the meantime, the Japanese resumed their air-raids on Rangoon, but once again the Allied fighter pilots provided such fierce and effective opposition that the attacks soon died away. Much attention has been paid to the Flying Tigers but it seems that the greatest credit should be given to the RAF's 17 and 135 (Hurricane) Squadrons and the finest individual achievement was that of Wing Commander Frank Carey, who personally shot down three enemy fighters on 26 February.

Of course the victories in the air could not balance the defeats inflicted on land. Hutton saw this clearly. Though he reorganized and reinforced 17th Indian Division and sent 7th Armoured Brigade forward to support it, he accepted that Rangoon was doomed. On 27 February, he ordered that the city be abandoned by 1 March after essential demolitions had been carried out, and that the British and Commonwealth troops should retire northward through the valley of the Irrawaddy River to avoid being cut off. He also turned back a convoy carrying 63rd Indian Brigade and 1st Indian Field Artillery Regiment to Burma, believing that these would merely provide a pointless sacrifice.

Dorman-Smith, with whom Hutton had discussed the situation fully, agreed with his judgement but Wavell, now in India after his ABDA Command had disintegrated, emphatically did not. He was furious to learn of Hutton's orders which he subsequently countermanded. Wavell's conduct strongly suggests that he too was suffering from strain and mental exhaustion. On 1 March he flew to Magwe airfield in central Burma, and here he stormed at the hapless Hutton in front of the governor, the Air Officer Commanding in Burma, Air Vice-Marshal Stevenson, and Hutton's own subordinates. Hutton retained his dignity and did not deign to reply, but he was to be further humiliated by being ordered to remain in Burma as his successor's chief of staff. He returned to India at his own request a month later and was not given another active command.

Wavell showed even less consideration for Smyth who, on 25 February, had unwisely written to Hutton requesting the two months' sick leave his medical board had recommended. Hutton, not knowing how ill Smyth really was, naturally felt that he had 'lost confidence in his ability to command'. Wavell agreed and on 1 March, appointed Cowan to replace Smyth as the leader of 17th Indian Division.

If this action was understandable, Wavell's subsequent treatment of Smyth was surely inexcusable. Both officers left Burma in a Blenheim bomber the next day, neither speaking a word to the other. On arrival at Calcutta, Wavell informed Smyth that he wished to proceed alone, whereupon Smyth's luggage was unceremoniously removed from the aircraft. When Smyth did reach New Delhi, he was greeted with the news that, on Wavell's instructions, he had been deprived of his acting rank of major general and compulsorily retired forthwith from the army. It was a sorry end to what had once been a brilliant military career.

At Calcutta, Wavell also met Alexander on his way to take up his command in Burma. Wavell ordered him to make 'every effort' to hold Rangoon but added that the Burma Army 'must not be allowed to be cut off and destroyed'. Alexander quickly realized that Rangoon could not be held and if he was to save his soldiers, he must get them out of the jaws of a fast-closing trap while there was still time. Luckily the Japanese, also obsessed with the importance of Rangoon, never appreciated that the Burma Army was in a trap. As a result, on 8 March there was presented the astonishing sight of the two sides' main formations racing parallel to each other but in different directions: Alexander made good his escape to the north and Iida stormed southward to the capture of the Burmese capital.

Rangoon's fall had been decided by the Battle of the Sittang River and since the Japanese could and did pour reinforcements into Rangoon's harbour, this battle may be said to have decided the fall of the rest of Burma as well. For Churchill, 23 February 1942 had brought the diplomatic disaster of the loss of Australian trust and confidence in Britain and the military disaster of the loss of another British colony. Perhaps his only consolation was the thought that surely even this worst of months could not possibly present him with any more bad news, but of course it could and did.

Notes

1. The Lysanders were supposed to be reconnaissance machines, but found themselves equipped with bombs and used to assist the efforts of the Blenheims.
2. By this time, an increasing number of officers in the Indian brigades were Indian, not British, and many distinguished themselves in the Burma campaigns. One of the defenders of Kuzeik was Captain Shri Kanth Korla whose gallantry won an immediate DSO. He later became a general in the army of an independent India. In the fight for the Sittang River bridge on 22 February, Captain Stephen Maneckshaw of 4/12th Frontier Force Regiment, although seriously wounded, won an immediate Military Cross. He later became India's first field marshal.
3. Brigadier Cowan's real Christian name was David but he was always known as 'Punch': he is supposed to have borne a resemblance to the puppet character.

Chapter 8

Slaughter in the Java Sea

B y nightfall on 23 February 1942, the month had seen Britain's army, Air Force, colonial administration and merchant marine all suffer heavy casualties, but those of the Royal Navy had been surprisingly light considering that the war had become almost literally worldwide. Even in the Channel Dash, despite the sacrifice of Esmonde's 825 Fleet Air Arm Squadron, the navy had not lost many men or much equipment: its loss had been that of prestige because of its failure to challenge the German battle-cruisers in its own home waters. On 24 February, however, a chain of events was started that would result in the sinking of several British and Commonwealth warships and the death or capture of many fine seamen.

The scene of this calamity would be the East Indies, where the Japanese were closing in on their greatest prize: the island of Java, rich in tea, coffee, rice, tobacco, coal, oil, gold, silver and tin. They had already prepared the way with a series of air attacks, one of which at Semplak in western Java on 22 February had destroyed a number of Allied aircraft on the ground and forced the abandonment of the airfield. It was clear that seaborne landings could not long be delayed, and indeed by the 24th, two enemy invasion fleets were already on their way.

When the ABDA Command had been set up in January 1942, the officer appointed to command the Allied Naval Forces – with the rather neat title of ABDAfloat – was the American Admiral Thomas Hart. It was not a wise choice, for Hart was an acerbic character who was not on good terms with his British and Dutch colleagues. Nor was he happy to be entrusted with the task of saving a European colonial empire of which, like most Americans, he did not approve.

Hart's attitude was understandably resented by the Dutch authorities, for many of whom the East Indies was and had always been their home – a factor that Hart failed to consider or appreciate – and who felt that in any case they should have more control over the defence of their possessions. Moreover, they had an eminently suitable candidate for the post of ABDAfloat in the person of Vice Admiral Conrad Helfrich, Commander-in-Chief of The Netherlands East Indies Forces, a determined, capable officer who had been born and brought up in the East Indies. The Netherlands government in exile in London and the Dutch ambassador in Washington strongly pressed for the removal of Hart, and on 12 February he was relieved, supposedly on account of ill health, and was duly replaced by Helfrich.

Under first Hart and then Helfrich came the ABDA Combined Striking Force, formed on 1 February, under the tactical command of the Dutch Rear Admiral Karel Doorman. In reality, though, ABDA's naval forces were not then combined. The British and Australian warships were normally based at Tanjong Priok, the port of Java's capital Batavia in the west of the island, where they were controlled by Commodore John Collins, the Australian senior naval officer in Batavia. The Dutch and American warships were usually to be found at Surabaya in the east of Java or at Tjilatjap on its south coast and came directly under Rear Admiral Doorman.

On 1 February, the Royal Navy at Tanjong Priok was represented by the heavy cruiser *Exeter*, the elderly First World War vintage light cruisers *Danae* and *Dragon* and a number of destroyers. Here they were soon to be joined by the Royal Australian Navy's more modern light cruisers *Perth* and *Hobart*. During most of the month, these vessels were employed on the important but unexciting task of providing the escort for Allied convoys.

Doorman's own force had more interesting and much more unpleasant experiences. These began in the early hours of 4 February, when it left Surabaya with the intention of intercepting a Japanese invasion convoy making for Makassar in the extreme south of Celebes. Doorman flew his flag in light cruiser *De Ruyter* and was accompanied by another Dutch light cruiser *Tromp*, US heavy cruiser *Houston*, US light cruiser *Marblehead*, and four American and three Dutch destroyers.

Sadly, none of these vessels came near the Makassar invasion convoy, which was thus able to complete Japan's conquest of southern Celebes unhindered. Instead, on the morning of 4 February Japanese aircraft from the aerodrome at Kendari on Celebes launched repeated attacks on Doorman's warships, forcing them to turn back after suffering considerable damage. A bomb hit on *De Ruyter* did little harm, but one on *Houston* struck her just forward of her rear turret which burst into flames, burning to death most of its crew and putting three of the cruiser's nine 8-inch guns permanently out of action. Nonetheless, *Houston* was able to remain with the ABDA Combined Striking Force, albeit with reduced fire-power.

Light cruiser *Marblehead* was still more unfortunate. Two direct hits and one very near miss left her circling helplessly with her steering gear out of action, listing, down by the bow with her after deck torn wide open and on fire. With her companions clustering protectively around her, she was able to make her way out of the danger zone but her damage was so great that, after temporary repairs had been carried out at Tjilatjap, she was withdrawn; first to Colombo, Ceylon where she was further repaired and eventually to the United States. It was some consolation that her casualty list was comparatively light: 15 killed and 34 injured compared with *Houston*'s 48 dead and 50 more wounded.

The depressing pattern of the Combined Striking Force's first mission would be followed in subsequent ones. All ended in failure and their only real result was the gradual but continuous reduction of Doorman's fighting strength. On 13 February, aerial reconnaissance reported the Japanese invasion convoy heading for Sumatra. Doorman hastily gathered together the largest force then available, but it was not until late on the 14th that it had all assembled and he could set out to intercept the troopships. His cruisers had increased in number, for although *Houston* and *Marblehead* were no longer with him, *De Ruyter* and *Tromp* had been reinforced permanently by another Dutch light cruiser, the appropriately-named *Java*, and temporarily by HMS *Exeter* and HMAS *Hobart*. Four Dutch and six American destroyers provided the escort.

That night, a freak accident robbed Doorman of two of his Dutch destroyers. As he approached Banka Island, the *Van Ghent* struck an uncharted reef and sank, and the *Banckert* was left behind to rescue survivors and take them back to Java.[1] Next day, Doorman's remaining vessels were subjected to continuous attacks by high-level bombers. These caused only minor damage with near misses, but that afternoon, with his ships' fuel and AA ammunition running low and no prospect of receiving any fighter cover, Doorman again abandoned an attempt to engage a Japanese invasion convoy.

It was a sad anti-climax and one that had brought the Striking Force west of Java at a moment when it would soon be required in waters east of that island. Furthermore, Doorman, with a number of different duties to perform, again dispersed his ships. *Exeter* and *Hobart* returned to their usual base at Tanjong Priok; Doorman went to Tjilatjap with *De Ruyter* and *Java*; *Tromp* went to Surabaya; and several destroyers remained in the vicinity of Sumatra, where on 17 February the Striking Force lost another Dutch destroyer, the *Van Nes*, sunk by Japanese bombers south of Banka Island while attempting to evacuate refugees.

Heavy cruiser *Houston* had not accompanied Doorman on this mission because on 14 February she had arrived at Port Darwin, accompanied by US destroyer *Peary*. On the following day, together with two Australian sloops, they formed the escort to that Allied troop convoy to Timor of which mention has already been made. As we have seen, air attacks forced this to turn back and on the 18th, *Houston* and *Peary* set out to rejoin Doorman. That night, however, a submarine was detected and *Peary* engaged in a long but unsuccessful hunt for it. This used up so much fuel that she had to return to Port Darwin for replenishment, just in time to be sunk by Nagumo's airmen on the 19th.

She was not the only Allied warship to suffer on this date. Early that morning, Japanese infantrymen poured ashore on Bali from two troopships anchored in the Badung Strait south-east of the island. Doorman's Striking Force was directed to attack them and since, as we have seen, his vessels were widely scattered, he decided not to waste time by concentrating them but to enter the Badung Strait in three separate waves. The first would consist of *De Ruyter*, *Java* and three destroyers, one Dutch and two American; the second of *Tromp* and four US destroyers; and the last of just eight Dutch motor-torpedo-boats.

Despite this dispersion of his strength – a dispersion increased by the three destroyers in his own group lagging well behind *De Ruyter* and *Java* – Doorman seemed certain to gain an easy morale-raising victory. One of the Japanese transports, the *Sagami Maru*,[2] had been badly damaged in a raid by Flying Fortresses but had been able to steam away that afternoon, escorted by destroyers *Arashio* and *Michishio*. The other troopship, the *Sasago Maru*, remained off Bali until after dark when she too set out under the protection of two more destroyers, *Asashio* and *Oshio*.

It was these three vessels that, at 2225, encountered *De Ruyter* and *Java*. There followed a series of frantic clashes in the dark, in which the Allied superiority in numbers and weight of gunfire was more than balanced by the Japanese superiority in accuracy of gunfire and their lethal liquid oxygen-powered 'Long Lance' torpedoes of which mention was made earlier. The first encounter, between the Dutch light cruisers and the Japanese destroyers, was indecisive: both sides fired ineffectively at long range, and then broke off the action by mutual consent.

Subsequent combats were fiercer and the Allied warships, attacking in their separate waves, had the worst of these. None of them sighted the vulnerable transport and the Dutch motor-torpedo-boats, the last vessels to reach the scene, failed to sight any enemy at all. The three destroyers that had been with *De Ruyter* and *Java* engaged *Asashio* and *Oshio* but did them no harm and lost the Dutch *Piet Hein*, struck by a Long Lance at 2240 and sinking soon afterwards with the loss of sixty-four of her crew.

In the early hours of 20 February, the *Tromp* group also clashed with *Asashio* and *Oshio*, inflicting minor injuries on both of them. The dauntless pair retaliated vigorously, no fewer than eleven shells hitting *Tromp* and causing severe damage to her superstructure. The leading US destroyer, the *Stewart*, also took at least two shell hits, resulting in damage and flooding. The American vessels were then engaged by *Arashio* and *Michishio* that had learned of what was taking place and returned to join in the fight. However, they proved less dangerous than their comrades and *Michishio* was struck by several shells that caused heavy casualties and for a time left her dead in the water, though she was later able to limp away to safety.

This belated success could not disguise the fact that Doorman's Striking Force had once again been repulsed. It had, moreover, been permanently deprived of the use of three of its number. *Piet Hein* had gone down. *Tromp* had to retire to Australia to make good her injuries. *Stewart*, on her return to Surabaya, was placed in dry dock so that her repairs could be carried out, but it seems she was not braced adequately for when the dock was raised, she capsized, wrecking it and damaging herself so badly that she was written off as a total loss.[3]

Since the Japanese capture of Bali followed hard on the heels of their conquest of Sumatra and was promptly followed in its turn by their invasion of Timor, Java was now menaced by enemies to the north, west and east, while Port Darwin, the base from which she might expect to receive supplies and reinforcements, had been put out of action. It was obvious that a Japanese assault on her must be imminent and indeed two powerful invasion fleets had already been prepared for landings in the north-west and north-east of Java simultaneously.

Both these invasions would be carried out by the men of Japan's Sixteenth Army, commanded by Lieutenant General Hitoshi Imamura and containing elements of four divisions. For the landings in the north-west of Java, Imamura had allocated his 2nd Infantry Division plus a regiment from 38th Division. These were carried in fifty-six transports and the intention was that the division should land at Bantam Bay to the west of Batavia and the regiment at Eretanwetan to the east of the capital; they would then move towards each other, thus overrunning western Java.

Protection of the troop transports was the responsibility of Vice Admiral Jisaburo Ozawa, a brave, capable officer who well before the war had championed the value of aircraft carriers but since its outbreak had been concerned mainly with amphibious operations, having commanded the naval forces that had supported Yamashita in

Malaya and subsequently those responsible for the invasion of Sumatra. In his Western Attack Group, he had light carrier *Ryujo*, heavy cruisers *Chokai* (his flagship), *Mogami*, *Mikuma*, *Suzuya* and *Kumano*, light cruisers *Natori* and *Yura*, seaplane tenders *Chitose* and *Mizuho* and nineteen destroyers. In addition, he could be supported, if required, by a reserve force under Vice Admiral Ibo Takahashi containing heavy cruisers *Ashigara* and *Myoko* and four more destroyers.

For north-eastern Java, Imamura had selected his 48th Infantry Division and the 56th Regimental Combat Group, the soldiers in which came mainly from 56th Division, hence the name. They would be taken to Rembang in forty-one transports and on landing the division would attack Surabaya, while 56th Regimental Combat Group would cross the island to its south coast and capture Tjilatjap.

These transports had been provided with a much less powerful escort, for Rear Admiral Shoji Nishimura's Eastern Attack Group at first contained only his flagship, light cruiser *Naka*, eight destroyers, four minesweepers and a few minor naval vessels. As the convoy entered the Java Sea, however, it was joined by light cruiser *Jintsu* and eight more destroyers under the command of Rear Admiral Raizo Tanaka who in the later Guadalcanal campaign would earn the open admiration of the Americans for his skill and determination. Once again the Japanese had provided a reserve, this one being commanded by Rear Admiral Takeo Takagi and containing heavy cruisers *Nachi* and *Haguro* and a pair of destroyers.

Vice Admiral Helfrich was made aware of the approach of both these convoys by aerial reconnaissance and made ready to resist them. It appeared to him that the Eastern Attack Force would arrive first and he was determined that the Combined Striking Force really would be combined for once and would oppose this as strongly as possible. On 24 February, therefore, he sent to Commodore Collins the signal that would direct British and Australian warships to leave Tanjong Priok for Surabaya where they would reinforce Doorman. A later signal gave a grim prophesy of their likely fate: 'Sacrifice is necessary for the defence of Java.'

At 1400 on 25 February, one Australian and four British warships set out for Surabaya, where they arrived on the afternoon of the

26th. Left behind at Tanjong Priok were four ancient British vessels, light cruisers *Danae* and *Dragon* and destroyers *Scout* and *Tenedos*. The Australian light cruiser *Hobart* had been one of those intended to join Doorman, but she was in urgent need of refuelling and was unable to comply. She and her elderly companions were therefore spared the fate of the vessels that went to Surabaya.[4]

Even without *Hobart*, the reinforcements made an impressive and encouraging sight, for they were fine ships with fine reputations. Heavy cruiser *Exeter* was rightly famous for her part in the Battle of the River Plate in December 1939 that had resulted in the destruction of the pocket battleship *Admiral Graf Spee*. Australian light cruiser *Perth* was also a veteran of a celebrated victory, the Battle of Matapan in March 1941, as was her skipper, Captain Hector Waller, who had there commanded a flotilla of destroyers and as a result of this and other services in the Mediterranean had earned the deep respect of all who knew him.

Commander Cecil Wakeford May, the senior officer in charge of the destroyers escorting *Exeter* and *Perth*, was also highly experienced. So was his ship, HMS *Electra*, though the experiences had not been pleasant ones. It was *Electra* that had rescued the only three survivors of battle-cruiser *Hood* when she was sunk by the *Bismarck* in May 1941, and she had later performed a similar task after the loss of *Prince of Wales* and *Repulse*. *Electra* was slightly larger and faster than Doorman's Dutch destroyers and larger, faster and better armed than the American ones. So was her sister ship *Encounter*, while the third destroyer, *Jupiter*, was larger still, more modern and better armed than the Dutch as well as the American destroyers.

Certainly Rear Admiral Doorman was delighted with these additions to his Striking Force, now stronger than it had ever been. Various problems with his destroyers meant that the American *Pope* and the Dutch *Evertsen* would not sail with him, and the speed of the Dutch *Kortenaer* – and so in practice the speed of the whole squadron – was restricted to 25 knots. Even so, Doorman now had two heavy cruisers, *Exeter* and *Houston*, three light cruisers, *De Ruyter*, *Java* and *Perth*, and nine destroyers, the British *Electra*, *Encounter* and *Jupiter*, the American *Alden*, *John D. Edwards*, *John D. Ford* and *Paul Jones*, and the Dutch *Kortenaer* and *Witte de With*.

Doorman also hoped to enjoy the benefit of fighter protection, for the old US aircraft carrier *Langley* had been ordered to Tjilatjap. She was no longer able to operate aircraft but she could transport them and she had on board thirty-two Kittyhawks. These were not in crates but assembled ready for flight immediately they were put ashore. However, in February 1942 little went right for the Allies and in the afternoon of the 27th, *Langley* and her precious Kittyhawks were sent to the bottom by Japanese shore-based bombers.

This meant that the Japanese retained their command of the air and their reconnaissance aircraft, in particular the float-planes carried by their cruisers, could and did keep a close watch on Doorman, while he remained largely in ignorance of their movements. As an additional handicap, because Doorman's Striking Force was composed of warships from nations without a common language, he had to carry on *De Ruyter* a British liaison officer who could translate his orders into English and signal these to *Exeter*, next in line behind the flagship; she then forwarded them to the other English-speaking vessels. This inevitably caused delays and made it difficult for Doorman to take any rapid action required.

None of these problems altered Doorman's resolve to engage his enemies. Spurred on by a signal from Helfrich to 'pursue attack until you have demolished Japanese force', he set out to seek for this in the evening of 26 February. As the Striking Force left Surabaya, *De Ruyter* collided with a tug and a water-barge, sinking them both. It was not a good beginning. To make sure that the Eastern Attack Force did not slip past him in the dark, Doorman spent the night steering close to the coast of Java. He thus made no contact with the Japanese who were still located well to the north.

Dawn on the 27th brought an air attack on destroyer *Jupiter* but happily this had no effect. There was still no sign of the Japanese so Doorman, ignoring orders from Helfrich, decided to return to Surabaya. He was just entering the swept channel between the minefields that guarded the port, when at 1427 he was advised that a reconnaissance aircraft had sighted large numbers of transports and their escorting warships some 80 miles to the north. He promptly reversed course, increased speed to 22 knots and made straight for the enemy.

Throughout the day, Doorman had been dogged by Japanese reconnaissance machines reporting his every movement. His latest change of course caused Rear Admiral Nishimura to become concerned for the safety of his troop convoy and to call on his colleagues for assistance. Rear Admiral Tanaka's force was already close at hand and Rear Admiral Takagi ordered his heavy cruisers *Nachi* and *Haguro* to steam at once to join Nishimura as well, when as the senior of the three Japanese flag officers, he would assume overall command. His flagship, *Nachi*, also catapulted a float-plane to keep track of Doorman. At 1500 it reported that the Combined Striking Force was heading directly towards the troopships. Nishimura ordered two of his destroyers to escort these away to the north, while the rest of the Japanese warships moved to intercept the Allied squadron.

Doorman had drawn up his cruisers in a single column, a somewhat inflexible formation but one perhaps best suited to a group of ships that were not used to operating together and were handicapped by communication problems; all they had to do was follow the flagship *De Ruyter*. Behind her came *Exeter*, then *Houston*, *Perth* and *Java* in that order. *Electra*, *Encounter* and *Jupiter* were on the starboard bow of the column, *Kortenaer* and *Witte de With* on its port beam and the four American destroyers on its port quarter.

These dispositions placed the three British destroyers nearest to the enemy warships, and at about 1605 Commander May sighted them and reported to his admiral. The Japanese squadrons lay to the north of Doorman who was approaching from the south-east. Nearest was Tanaka with light cruiser *Jintsu* and eight destroyers, while Nishimura with light cruiser *Naka* and six destroyers was still further north. The Japanese spotted the Combined Striking Force at the same moment that it had seen them, and immediately afterwards both sides, with very different feelings, detected a new group of warships: Takagi's *Nachi* and *Haguro*, an impressive sight with huge white waves curling away from their bows as they raced to join the fight at a speed of over 30 knots.

At 1616 the Japanese heavy cruisers opened fire and the series of clashes that together made up the Battle of the Java Sea had begun. Takagi enjoyed an immediate positional advantage because the Japanese warships were all on a westward course that took them in front of the Allied column. This meant that they could fire their full broadsides, while Doorman's vessels could use only their forward guns in reply: a manoeuvre known for obvious reasons as 'crossing the T'.

Realizing his danger, at 1621 Doorman swung his column 20 degrees to port. This put him on a course roughly parallel to that of his enemies but gradually closing the distance between them. It also, unfortunately, was a course that took him ever further away from that troop convoy he was so desperate to engage and the Japanese were so determined to protect.

Doorman's turn did enable *Exeter* and *Houston* to direct the fire of all their guns onto their opponents but the Combined Striking Force was still at a considerable disadvantage. Since *Houston*'s rear turret was still inoperable, both the Allied heavy cruisers had only six 8-inch guns, whereas *Nachi* and *Haguro* had ten. Nor could Doorman's light cruisers help because the range was too great for their 6-inch weapons. Similarly, on the starboard bow of the cruiser column, the British destroyers were coming under fire from Tanaka's *Jintsu* but were unable to retaliate. Moreover, the Japanese now had three float-planes reporting their fall of shot, since *Naka* and *Jintsu* had launched their aircraft to assist the one from *Nachi*.

Despite these benefits, the Japanese achieved little for some time. *Jintsu*'s fire straddled *Electra* but caused no damage. The heavy cruisers scored repeated near misses, *Perth* being straddled by eight salvoes in succession, but they inflicted only minor damage, on *Exeter* with a near miss close astern, and on *De Ruyter* with the only shell to score a hit during this part of the battle and it passed through her deck into an auxiliary engine-room but failed to explode.

Nor were Japanese torpedoes any more effective at this stage. Starting at about 1633, Nishimura's squadron launched forty-three of them but happily at a distance too great even for the 'Long Lance'. Nishimura's destroyers did, however, hamper the Allied gunners still more by laying down a smokescreen as they retired. If the Japanese had so far been unable to inflict any real damage, neither had the Allied warships.

Then at 1708, Tanaka's *Jintsu* fired torpedoes at the Allied line, her example being followed by her accompanying destroyers; one of these, the *Tokitsukaze*, had been hit as she approached and was pouring out clouds of thick white smoke, but was still able to carry out her attack. *Nachi* and *Haguro* launched torpedoes at the same time. Yet it was their gunfire that proved most significant. They had not been hindered by the smokescreen thanks to the good work of their spotting aircraft, and at 1708 the luck of the Combined Striking Force ran out.

A deafening roar of escaping steam revealed that *Exeter* had been hit. An 8-inch shell had plunged into her boiler-room, killing fourteen men, causing a temporary loss of power that put her main armament out of action and destroying six of her eight boilers. As her speed fell away, first to 11 and then to only 5 knots, Captain Oliver Gordon, fearing that his ship would be run down by *Houston* next astern of her, ordered a hasty turn to port. The three cruisers following *Exeter* concluded that her move had been ordered by Doorman as a means of avoiding torpedoes, so also turned to port. *De Ruyter* and the three British destroyers, thus left dangerously isolated, had no choice but to change course also. The Allied formation had disintegrated.

While all was still confusion, another blow fell on Doorman's squadron. A Long Lance struck destroyer *Kortenaer* and literally tore her in half. The two halves rose high into the air while her crew scrambled onto life-rafts; then they slowly sank, leaving her survivors alone in a sea fouled by oil and wreckage.

Exeter could almost be considered fortunate by comparison. Desperate efforts by her damage-control parties extinguished fires that had been started and enabled her to regain the use of her guns and increase her speed, though only to 15 knots. Captain Waller, who had been the first to appreciate that *Exeter* was in trouble, took *Perth* between her and her enemies and endeavoured to shield her with a smokescreen. Nonetheless, it was clear to all that she was still very vulnerable and in considerable peril.

At first the Japanese had also believed that the Allied turn to port had been a deliberate tactic to evade their torpedoes and many of them, rather ironically, mentally congratulated their opponents on their skill. However, reports from their float-planes quickly made it clear that the Combined Striking Force was in a state of confusion and Rear Admiral Takagi ordered another torpedo attack that he hoped might complete its destruction.

Fortunately, Rear Admiral Doorman appreciated Takagi's intentions and the danger they posed to *Exeter* in particular. He signalled: 'All ships follow me'; then led his squadron between *Exeter* and the enemy. On learning the full extent of *Exeter*'s injuries, he ordered Captain Gordon to return to Surabaya with destroyer *Witte de With* to escort her.[5] At about 1725, he instructed the British destroyers to cover *Exeter*'s retreat by counter-attacking.

Commander May responded immediately. Without waiting for *Encounter* and *Jupiter*, both of which were well to the south of him, he took *Electra* through the smokescreen only to be confronted with a whole succession of enemies looming out of the haze, for both Nishimura and Tanaka were trying to get at the Allied cruisers. Exactly what happened is not clear but it seems that *Electra* exchanged fire with destroyer *Asagumo*, scoring a hit on her that killed five men, wounded another nineteen and left her temporarily dead in the water, though she was later able to limp away. In return, however, *Asagumo* made two hits on *Electra* that put her after boiler-room out of action. She, too, slowed to a halt.

Electra was now an easy target. Destroyer *Minegumo* poured a torrent of shells into her but May fought back as best he could, not only with gunfire but also with a salvo of torpedoes that, sadly, missed their target. Other enemy destroyers then appeared, and under constant fire *Electra*'s guns were knocked out one after the other and she began to list to port and slowly sink. 'Abandon Ship' was ordered and at about 1800 *Electra* disappeared bows first beneath the Java Sea. Commander May went down with her but in the early hours of the following day fifty-four survivors were rescued by US submarine *S-38*. It is reported that one man, Able Seaman Benjamin Roberts, who was not on a life-raft but swimming on his own in a life-jacket, could not at first be located in the darkness but he called out to the submarine's crew to leave him and make sure they saved his companions. They did so and, happily, they also found and saved Able Seaman Roberts.

Encounter and *Jupiter* subsequently engaged enemy warships before turning back into the smokescreen, no damage being suffered by either side. *Exeter* by this time had retired and Doorman led the rest of his cruiser force eastward and later southward, his intention being to escape contact with Takagi's forces and then circle round them to find the elusive troop convoy. *Nachi* and *Haguro* continued to fire on the Striking Force but Japanese shells do not seem to have been very reliable in this battle for although two hit *Houston* neither of them exploded. Another torpedo attack by Nishimura's squadron made no hits at all.

At about 1815, in the gathering dusk, Doorman signalled to the four US destroyers: 'Cover my retirement.' It appears that he meant them to hide him from Japanese eyes by making smoke. They, however, felt that the best way of protecting their cruisers was by a torpedo attack on *Nachi* and *Haguro*. This failed to score any hits but persuaded Takagi to break off the action. Since the American warships now had no torpedoes left and were becoming desperately short of fuel, Doorman ordered them to withdraw to Surabaya shortly afterwards.

The sun set at 1821 and some twenty minutes later, Doorman turned to the north-west, still hoping to encounter the elusive troop convoy. Instead, at 1927 he encountered *Nachi* and *Haguro*. These were in fact at a grave disadvantage as both were dead in the water while *Nachi* recovered her float-plane. They hastily got under way, putting out a smokescreen and firing star-shells to illuminate the Allied warships. There was a brief exchange of gunfire before, at 1936, the aggressive Tanaka led his squadron into yet another torpedo attack that scored no hits but ensured that Doorman once more retired.

Doorman's every attempt to find the Japanese invasion force had been thwarted. Unaware that this had been kept well to the north out of trouble, he felt that it might have outflanked him and already be closing in on Java. He therefore took his Striking Force back to the island and steamed westward along its northern shore. Doorman's destroyer escort was now down to the British pair *Encounter* and *Jupiter* and before he sighted the enemy again, he was to be deprived of the services of both of them.

At 2125 a violent explosion lit up the night and HMS *Jupiter* signalled: 'I am torpedoed.' In fact she had hit a mine that had apparently drifted from a minefield laid earlier that day by the Dutch. Water poured into *Jupiter*'s engine-room, bringing her to a halt. In accordance with previous instructions, her companions pressed on without her. Determined work by her damage-control parties was able to keep her afloat for four hours, giving her crew plenty of time to abandon her. Seventy-eight of them managed to reach the coast of Java in lifeboats, while others, including Lieutenant Commander Thew, were picked up by the Japanese to become prisoners of war.

Doorman then turned north in a last attempt to find the invasion convoy. At 2217 life-rafts were sighted: by sheer chance the Combined Striking Force had reached the position in which *Kortenaer* had gone down. Destroyer *Encounter* was detached to assist survivors and rescued 113 of them whom she then carried to Surabaya.

The four Allied cruisers continued unescorted, but their task was a hopeless one. Captain Waller would later pay tribute to the enemy's 'most superbly organized air reconnaissance' and this continued even after dark, the Japanese airmen dropping flares to illuminate the Allied warships and reporting their every move to Takagi. At about 2300 Doorman again sighted Japanese ships, but they were not the troop transports as he had hoped but *Nachi*, *Haguro*, *Jintsu* and eight destroyers.

By this time, both sides were becoming exhausted and although a bright moon provided reasonable visibility, Allied and Japanese gunnery alike proved inaccurate and ineffective but at 2322 *Nachi* launched eight Long Lances and *Haguro* another four. The Imperial Navy's 'secret weapons' had so far proved surprisingly disappointing. Now they justified the confidence that had been placed in them. Both *De Ruyter* and *Java* were struck, burst into spectacular and inextinguishable flames, came to a halt and sank; the latter in just fifteen minutes, the former some time later. Rear Admiral Doorman went down with his flagship, his last signal to *Perth* and *Houston* being an order to save themselves and not risk destruction by trying to rescue survivors.

So ended the Battle of the Java Sea and with it all possibility of preventing the Japanese conquest of Java. The remaining Allied ships were concerned only with leaving the area, not with opposing the enemy landings. During the evening of 28 February, the Eastern Attack Force was engaged north of Rembang but only by the obsolete Vildebeests of 36 Squadron RAF; they did no damage and Squadron Leader Wilkins failed to return. Japanese soldiers duly landed at Rembang and at the same time the Western Attack Force put its troops ashore at Bantam Bay and Eretanwetan. The former move had an additional if unintended result, for it blocked the Sunda Strait between Java and Sumatra through which most of the survivors of the Combined Striking Force planned to make their escape.

There were two main groups of survivors, one at Tanjong Priok, the other at Surabaya. *Perth* and *Houston* had reached Tanjong Priok at 1400 on 28 February and there they found the Dutch destroyer *Evertsen* that had been sent there from Surabaya earlier. Vice Admiral Helfrich was still full of fight and determined to re-form his Striking Force at Tjilatjap. On his orders, *Perth* and *Houston* set out for the Sunda Strait on the evening of the 28th. *Evertsen* was not then ready to leave but followed them soon afterwards.

For most of 27 February, the ships of the Combined Striking Force had hunted for a Japanese invasion fleet but in vain. Now at about 2315 on the 28th, *Perth* and *Houston* in Bantam Bay did find the Western Attack Force and this was extremely vulnerable with bright moonlight illuminating the scene, the transports disembarking their troops, the Japanese covering forces some way to the north, only one destroyer, the *Fubuki*, watching the entrance to the bay and only two others, *Harukaze* and *Hatakaze*, guarding the troopships. It was a cruel irony.

The Japanese destroyers went into action with admirable promptness, the two with the transports hastily laying down a smokescreen and *Fubuki* sending up a star-shell to reveal the position of *Perth* and *Houston*. Captain Waller opened fire on her, whereupon she retaliated by launching nine torpedoes, but on this occasion the extraordinary range of the Long Lances proved a disadvantage to their own creators. The Allied cruisers evaded them by turning sharply to starboard and they ran on towards the troopships, two of them striking and sinking the *Sakura Maru*.

Next *Perth* and *Houston* shelled the unlucky transports, damaging three of them so badly that they had to be beached to stop them sinking as well. One of these was *Ryujo Maru* carrying Lieutenant General Imamura and the staff of his Sixteenth Army. Imamura was blown overboard and finally got ashore three hours later, exhausted, covered with oil and clinging to a piece of driftwood.

By 2340, however, the Japanese covering forces, in response to frantic signals, had arrived to support *Harukaze* and *Hatakaze*, already bravely engaging the Allied cruisers with gunfire and torpedoes. Ferociously attacked by heavy cruisers *Mogami* and *Mikuma*, light cruiser *Natori* and a further seven destroyers, *Perth* and *Houston* fought back desperately. They scored hits on *Mikuma*, *Harukaze* and another destroyer, *Shirakumo* – though only *Harukaze*, with three men killed, five wounded and her rudder temporarily jammed, suffered any real harm – but the odds against them were too great.

Perth sank first, five minutes after midnight, struck by countless shells and at least two, probably four Long Lances. Captain Waller and 352 of his men were killed and 100 more perished in prisoner of war camps, only 229 returning to Australia. *Houston* battled on for another forty-five minutes before at least twenty shells and at least three, perhaps six torpedoes combined to send her to the bottom. Captain Rooks and 637 others died in action, 104 more died in captivity and only 266 came home at the end of the war.

Had Dutch destroyer *Evertsen* accompanied *Perth* and *Houston*, her fate would undoubtedly have been the same and as it was, this was only briefly postponed. She witnessed the encounter of *Perth* and *Houston* with the Western Attack Force in Bantam Bay and avoided this dangerous area, but in the early hours of 1 March she was detected by a pair of Japanese destroyers. Seven shell-hits set her on fire and so damaged her that in order to avoid sinking she was forced to run herself aground on an islet, where she became a total loss.

During that same night, British Blenheims and Australian Hudsons made spirited raids on the landings at Bantam Bay and Eretanwetan and in the morning twelve Hurricanes made low-level strafing attacks at Eretanwetan, inflicting considerable losses on soldiers coming ashore in landing craft as well as setting three light tanks on fire. Such minor episodes, however, could not hope to check the Japanese. By 6 March, all RAF Blenheims and Vildebeests had been destroyed and the three remaining Hudsons were evacuated to Australia. The sturdy Hurricanes fought on until 8 March, when the only two survivors had to be destroyed on the ground. On the 8th also, the Dutch commander in Java, Lieutenant General ter Poorten, began negotiations for a surrender and hostilities ceased at noon the next day.

Prior to this, February 1942 had seen the beginning of another tragedy for Britain and one that would deal another blow to Churchill personally. After the Battle of the Java Sea, *Exeter*, *Encounter* and the four American destroyers had returned to Surabaya where they were joined by another US destroyer, the *Pope*, the engine-room troubles that had kept her out of the conflict now rectified. Clearly these vessels could not remain at Surabaya and on 28 February, all the American warships except *Pope* passed through the Bali Strait between that island and Java, ultimately reaching Australia safely.

As they left, the American sailors cheered *Exeter*, knowing that she could not follow them through the narrow Bali Strait without the risk of grounding in its shallow waters. It was suggested that she might use the Lombok Strait further east, but this was rejected for fear of attack by bombers based on Bali. Captain Gordon was therefore ordered to make a wide sweep towards the south coast of Borneo in order to avoid detection and then proceed through the Sunda Strait where the presence of the Japanese had not then been reported.

During her brief stay in harbour, *Exeter*'s engine-room personnel had worked tirelessly to repair her injuries and enable her to steam at 23 knots. At 1900 on 28 February, she set out on her last voyage. USS *Pope*, being the only American destroyer that still carried torpedoes, had been instructed to help protect her, as had HMS *Encounter* from which the Dutch survivors whom she had rescued from the Java Sea had now been put ashore.

Exeter and her faithful destroyers were not sighted during the hours of darkness, but daylight brought enemy reconnaissance aircraft that reported their presence to Takagi and also to Vice Admiral Takahashi whose reserve force had so far seen no action, a situation that he was eager to rectify. At 0935 *Exeter*'s old opponents *Nachi* and *Haguro*, accompanied by destroyers *Yamakaze* and *Kawakaze*, appeared to the south. Immediately afterwards, to the west of and directly ahead of *Exeter*, Takahashi's squadron came into view: heavy cruisers *Ashigara* and *Myoko* and destroyers *Ikazuchi* and *Akebono*.

As *Encounter* and *Pope* laid down a smokescreen, *Exeter* turned back to the east but she had no chance of escaping. By 1000 there were Japanese warships on both her flanks: *Nachi*, *Haguro* and all the enemy destroyers to starboard; *Ashigara* and *Myoko* to port. Aided by three float-planes circling overhead to direct their fall of shot, the four Japanese cruisers delivered a heavy and accurate cross-fire, scoring an early hit that wrecked *Exeter*'s fire control system and repeated near misses that caused further damage.

Exeter retaliated with every weapon at her command. She launched six torpedoes at *Ashigara* and *Myoko*, though without success; her main armament fired continuously, and her AA gunners, not to be outdone, opened up at the Japanese float-planes whenever opportunity offered. Yet it was obvious that it could only be a question of time before she suffered a disabling wound, and at 1120 this was inflicted. As in the Java Sea, an 8-inch shell found a boiler-room, reducing her speed to a mere 4 knots. Thus crippled, she made an easy target for a hail of shells that knocked out all her guns, set her on fire and brought her to a halt. At 1130 Captain Gordon ordered: 'Abandon Ship'. As her crew scrambled clear of her, *Ikazuchi* and *Akebono* dashed in to fire eighteen Long Lances. Several of these struck home and at 1140, *Exeter* rolled over and sank by the stern.

Meanwhile, *Ashigara* and *Myoko* had turned their fire onto *Encounter*. She, too, was hit repeatedly and brought to a halt, on fire and with her engine-room flooded. Lieutenant Commander Morgan made a quick tour of his destroyer and 'satisfied myself that there was nothing further to be done, and that the ship was sinking.' He gave the order to abandon her and at 1145, she also went down. *Pope* escaped destruction for a time by taking refuge in a convenient rain squall, but when she emerged from this, she was attacked by aircraft from light carrier *Ryujo*. These made several near misses that caused severe flooding and left her slowly sinking by the stern. The Japanese heavy cruisers finished her off.

It was not until the following morning that the survivors of the British warships were taken aboard Japanese destroyers. Captain Gordon, Lieutenant Commander Morgan, fifty other officers and 750 seamen were carried to prisoner of war camps. Japanese contempt for those who surrendered made these dubious refuges and though at first the enemy freely acknowledged the courage and determination shown by the crews of *Exeter* and *Encounter*, as the long months of war dragged on, this was gradually forgotten by their captors and 152 of them did not live to witness the end of hostilities.

This then was the latest bad news to reach Churchill. On the previous day, he had for a wonder received some encouragement: a small but brilliantly-executed Commando raid on Bruneval in northern France had seized an example of the latest German radar equipment, knowledge of which would greatly assist future British aerial operations. It might be thought that Churchill would at least have mentioned this in his letter to Roosevelt of 5 March but he did not do so, and it appears that any satisfaction it may have given him could not lift the gloom induced by the sinking of *Exeter*, the loss of which he seems to have felt deeply.

Nor was this surprising. In December 1939 *Exeter*, accompanied by two light cruisers, HMS *Ajax* and HMNZS *Achilles*, had engaged the pocket battleship *Admiral Graf Spee* near the mouth of the River Plate and driven her to seek shelter in Montevideo, where she was later scuttled. *Exeter* had been heavily damaged in this action. Burning, listing heavily, her steering gear crippled and all her 8-inch guns out of action, she had made her way painfully to the nearest British base, the Falkland Islands, where it was proposed she should remain for the rest of the war, so great were her injuries.

Churchill, who was then First Lord of the Admiralty, would have none of this. He insisted that *Exeter* be brought back to Britain and restored to her full fighting capability and when *Exeter* finally reached Plymouth in February 1940, he was there to meet her and praise her gallant crew. He declared with truth that: 'The brilliant

action in which you played a memorable part, came like a flash of
light and colour on the scene, carrying with it an encouragement to
ourselves and to our Allies.'

Exeter indeed had become more than just a ship. Her durability,
proved by her having got home despite her tremendous punishment,
made as great an impression as the skill and courage of her crew. She
stood as a symbol of Britain's determination to fight on whatever the
odds and Britain's capacity to endure suffering and loss and still
survive. Now this ship with which Churchill had been so closely
associated, this symbol that had meant so much to him, was gone
forever. No wonder Churchill was despondent.

Notes

1. *Banckert* therefore missed the action in the Badung Strait that Doorman was
shortly to fight. She would also miss the Battle of the Java Sea but for a more
sinister reason: on 24 February, an air-raid on Surabaya scored a very near miss
that tore a huge hole in her stern and disabled her. On 2 March, the Dutch
scuttled her to prevent her falling into enemy hands.
2. The word 'maru' included in the names of Japanese merchantmen was one
that had been added to the names of aristocrats' sons in Japan's feudal age. To
give it to a ship implies that this has a personality, much as Europeans or
Americans call a vessel not 'it' but 'she'.
3. *Stewart* was clearly a tough customer for, despite this mishap and attempts
to destroy her with scuttling charges on 2 March, she was not in fact a total
loss. A year later, the Japanese repaired her, rearmed her and on 15 June 1943
added her to the Imperial Navy as a patrol boat with the unromantic name of
No. 102. She survived the war and returned to the United States. She was
finally sunk by being used as a target for naval gunfire on 24 May 1946.
4. On both 26 and 27 February the warships at Tanjong Priok put to sea in
search of the Western Attack Force but, luckily for them, failed to find it. On
the 28th, Helfrich ordered them to retire to Ceylon.
5. *Witte de With* thus took no further part in the Battle of the Java Sea, but this
did not enable her to escape the curse that seems to have been laid on all Dutch
destroyers in the East Indies. On 1 March she was badly damaged by an air-
raid on Surabaya and the Dutch scuttled her on the following day.

Chapter 9

Further Forfeits

Not only did the events of February 1942 provide Britain with an unending succession of bad news, they also ensured there would be more trouble in the future. The Royal Navy remained tied down watching the *Tirpitz* while the U-boats continued their destruction of merchant shipping, particularly in the western Atlantic. February 1942 had seen the war's highest losses so far, but the 85 ships then sunk rose to 95 in March, fell slightly to 74 in April, then rose again to 125 in May, 144 in June and 96 in July. The tonnage lost in each of these months was well over 400,000 and in June it was a record 700,235. Well might Captain Roskill remark that 'in the first seven months of 1942, the enemy had reason to be satisfied over the achievements of his U-boats.'

The U-boats presented a continuous danger in the Atlantic, but the Axis threat in the Mediterranean was more immediate. In his diary for 16 February, Brooke recorded the fall of Singapore, the danger to Rangoon, the discontent caused by the Channel Dash and, equally serious, the loss or repulse of the 'three transports trying to reinforce Malta' in Convoy MW9. Both Brooke and Churchill knew that Malta was crucial for success in the Mediterranean and during the months that followed February 1942, her survival remained very doubtful.

Since the Axis commanders were equally aware of the importance of Malta and the need to prevent her receiving supplies, they would subject the next convoy attempting to reach her to attacks by both naval and air forces. Convoy MW10, which left Alexandria for Malta on 20 March, contained the Royal Navy Auxiliary supply ship

Breconshire and three merchantmen, one of them *Clan Campbell*, the sole transport to have survived MW9. It seems, though, that her bomb damage on that occasion had not been fully rectified, for her speed was reduced and she lagged behind the convoy, eventually being ordered to steam straight ahead while the other ships zigzagged.

On 22 March a strong Italian fleet attempted to get at the convoy, but was held off by the bold and brilliant counter-attacks of its greatly outnumbered escorts. The Italians were not wholly unsuccessful, however, since they caused the convoy to be diverted to the south and it was therefore unable to reach Malta under cover of darkness as planned. Heavy raids by enemy bombers on the morning of the 23rd sank the luckless *Clan Campbell* and disabled *Breconshire*; the latter was towed to a harbour on the south side of Malta, where she eventually capsized after numerous further attacks. The *Pampas* and the Norwegian *Talabot* did reach Grand Harbour, Valletta, but Field Marshal Kesselring directed every Stuka and Junkers Ju 88 that he had available against them in an onslaught that lasted for three days and finally sank them both. Of the 26,000 tons of supplies that had left Alexandria, just 5,000 tons were unloaded.

It was not until mid-June that another convoy could be sent to the aid of Malta, but then it was decided to dispatch two, one from Alexandria and one from Gibraltar, in the hope that this would divide the enemy's attention and resources. The two parts of the convoy from Alexandria, together known by the code name VIGOROUS and containing eleven merchantmen in all, set out in the evening of 11 June and at noon on the 12th. Also on the 12th, the five freighters and the American tanker *Kentucky* that formed the HARPOON convoy passed through the Straits of Gibraltar and headed towards Malta from the west.

Force H, now commanded by a South African officer, Vice Admiral Sir Neville Syfret, provided the escort for HARPOON, though its main strength including aircraft carriers *Eagle* and *Argus* would accompany the merchantmen only as far as The Narrows between Sicily and Cape Bon, Tunisia. It would then turn back at dusk on 14 June, leaving the convoy to pass through The Narrows at night before making a final dash for Malta. During the 14th, the handful of Sea Hurricanes and Fulmars on the two carriers beat off numerous attacks and only one merchant ship was sunk. Next day, in the absence of the Fleet Air Arm fighters, three more were lost including the precious tanker, but two – *Troilus* and *Orari* – reached Malta safely in the early hours of the 16th, their 15,000 tons of food and ammunition providing a breathing space for the battered island fortress.

It was little more than this, however, for by that time it was known that no more supplies would reach Malta before August at the earliest. The VIGOROUS convoy had no accompanying aircraft carrier. It was for a time protected by Hurricanes and Kittyhawks operating at long range from bases in the Western Desert. These thwarted a number of air attacks but as the convoy continued westward, the loss of the Martuba airfields again exerted its sinister influence. The Hurricanes and Kittyhawks disappeared and the Junkers Ju 87s and Ju 88s returned in full strength.

By the late afternoon of 14 June, the convoy had reached Bomb Alley and here it was threatened not only by air attacks but also by a powerful Italian surface force. Happily this never made contact, but conflicting reports of its progress kept the convoy steering backwards and forwards throughout 15 June. By that evening, two of the merchantmen had been sunk and two more had turned back, badly damaged. Worse still, the escorting warships had expended more than two-thirds of their anti-aircraft ammunition and if they advanced further in the face of such continuous air-raids as those they had been experiencing, this would soon be exhausted. The convoy returned to Alexandria.

Malta's situation had now become desperate. The already scanty rations of food, issued to the fighting services and civilians alike, were cut to an absolute minimum and already unpleasant skin diseases caused by malnutrition were starting to appear. Military stores such as ammunition and aviation fuel had to be tightly controlled. So to an even greater extent did kerosene, source of all heat and light on a treeless island, and oil, source of all power for everything from flour mills through pumps drawing water from the deep wells to cranes in the harbour. Such was the shortage of fuel that General Lord Gort VC, who had succeeded Lieutenant General

Dobbie as governor on 7 May, had to travel through Valletta on a bicycle.

Once Malta had used up these essential commodities, she would have no option but to surrender, thereby leaving the way clear for the Axis powers to pour supplies across the Mediterranean virtually unhindered. As it was, Malta was so handicapped by the restrictions imposed on her that the enemy was able to get a major convoy through to North Africa in March 1942, two more in April and another in May. In Cyrenaica by late May, four large ammunition dumps, 11,000 tons of fuel and enough food to supply Panzerarmee Afrika for thirty days had been accumulated, ready for a new Axis offensive.

Only in one respect did Malta receive a benefit in early 1942. By the end of April, the Germans badly needed aircraft to make good shortages in both Russia and North Africa. Encouraged by Malta's comparative lack of effectiveness, they found their replacements by transferring the bulk of Kesselring's bombers to these areas, thereby easing his direct assaults on the island. It would soon be learned, however, that Malta's advantage was Eighth Army's misfortune.

That General Auchinleck, as we have noted, 'entirely failed' to appreciate Malta's importance was a major cause of his steadily worsening relationship with both Churchill and Brooke. Their signals to him became ever more impatient and demanding and Auchinleck, who had an almost morbid hatred of criticism, became increasingly disheartened as a result. It was not a good preparation for meeting the attack on the Gazala Line that Rommel would launch late on 26 May.

Yet there seemed no reason for the British to be concerned. They had been warned of Rommel's intentions by Ultra, whereas German Intelligence had failed to uncover the details of Eighth Army's strong defensive positions. On paper Rommel had five infantry divisions to Eighth Army's four, but in reality his four Italian ones were under strength and lacking in motor vehicles, so only the German 90th Light Division could play an effective role in the coming action. On paper the supporting air-arms were roughly equal in strength, but in practice the Italian warplanes that made up about half of the Axis numbers took little part in the fighting.

Eighth Army's greatest advantage lay in the strength of its armour. Rommel controlled 560 tanks but 228 of these were the useless Italian ones and only 242 of his panzers were Mark IIIs, though all of these had now been fitted with the additional frontal armour protection. Furthermore, some of them were new Mark III Specials with 50mm front armour – but only 30mm armour on their sides and their turrets – and a new long-barrelled high-velocity 50mm gun that gave them a weapon superior to that of any Allied tank previously in use. Fortunately, when the Battle of Gazala began there were only nineteen of them on hand and as late as 10 June this had increased to only twenty-seven.

By contrast, Eighth Army had 850 tanks in the front line, as many as 167 of which were the new American Grants. These could boast 50mm of armour on the front of the hull, 57mm on the turret and 38mm side plates. Even at close range they had little to fear from the standard German tanks, whose crews in the Battle of Gazala would watch in horror as their shells literally bounced off the Grants' armour. In addition, the Grants carried not only a 37mm gun in the turret, but a 75mm one in a sponson on the hull. This latter had a limited traverse, but could fire either high-explosive shells at non-armoured targets or armour-piercing shells with an even greater penetrative power than those fired by the guns of the Mark III Specials.

Nor was the Grant the only new weapon with which Eighth Army had been equipped. It had also received 6-pounder anti-tank guns that were considerably superior to the German 50mms and about equal to the captured Russian 76mms that were just reaching Rommel. The Germans' 88mms were still the most deadly of all anti-tank guns, but Panzerarmee Afrika had only forty-eight of these while Eighth Army had 112 6-pounders.

Unfortunately, British errors more than outweighed British material advantages. Every fault that should have become apparent earlier in the year had remained unrectified and was repeated: the dispersal of infantry and artillery, though, ironically, at several crucial moments Rommel's panzers were far more widely dispersed than the British tanks; constant attacks straight into the muzzles of anti-tank guns; distrust between different formations and branches of the army; 'indiscipline at the top'; Auchinleck's attempts to control the battle from Cairo; and Churchill's attempts to influence it from London. In consequence, although the battle started off well for Eighth Army, it soon went badly wrong and ended in spectacular defeat.

By 14 June Eighth Army was falling back from the Gazala Line. It had previously been agreed that should this happen, the next defensive position would be on the Egyptian frontier; there would be no second siege of Tobruk. Auchinleck, however, now came under strong pressure from Churchill not to abandon a town that was a valuable port, an important base and a symbol of determined British resistance. He decided to defend it after all, but by 18 June Rommel had swung south of Tobruk, the coastal road east of it had been cut and its garrison had been isolated from the rest of Eighth Army.

Worse still, Rommel had seized the forward airfields of the Desert Air Force, compelling it to operate from aerodromes almost 200 miles further east. It was therefore impossible for its fighters to reach Tobruk without long-range fuel tanks, of which very few were readily available. The Germans' transfer to North Africa of bombers previously pounding Malta was now dramatically rewarded. Early on the morning of 20 June, Kesselring hurled every aircraft he could muster into a massive bombardment of Tobruk's defences. Flying without interference apart from AA fire, delighted that they 'had no *Huren-kähne* to harass them', the German warplanes stunned the defenders and enabled the German soldiers to break into the town. The Stukas then made repeated attacks on British headquarters and acted as 'flying artillery' for their ground troops.

Early on the 21st, the main part of the Tobruk garrison surrendered, though some smaller units did not follow suit until the 22nd. A few brave individuals did not surrender at all and broke out of the trap to make their way to the British lines. However, the Germans captured 32,000 British or Commonwealth soldiers, guns, ammunition, 5,000 tons of food, 2,000 serviceable vehicles and 1,400 tons of petrol. It was the largest British capitulation of the war, apart from that at Singapore.

When the news reached Britain, public indignation that had previously erupted in February over the Channel Dash flared up again. In a by-election at Maldon in Essex, a massive 'protest vote' decisively rejected a candidate from Churchill's National Government. In the House of Commons a motion was tabled on 25 June expressing 'no confidence in the central direction of the war'. It seems that Churchill did not feel that the motion posed any great threat to his own position, though he deplored the impression it might give and the effect it might produce abroad, and he would meet it with courage and resolution. The obvious lack of confidence in the country as a whole, however, understandably worried him and must surely have added to his burdens.

Yet it may be that Churchill was fortunate in having to direct his attention to so many problems close to home, because these distracted his attention from the calamities occurring in the Far East and the profound results that these would ultimately bring. That there would be more bad news from the Far East after February 1942 was certain. As already mentioned, the disaster at the Sittang River bridge had ensured the fall of Rangoon, and the disaster in the Java Sea had guaranteed the fall of Java. By early March, both had duly been lost and the torrent of misfortunes showed no sign of slackening.

In early April, two Japanese fleets moved into the Indian Ocean. Vice Admiral Ozawa with light carrier *Ryujo*, five heavy cruisers, one light cruiser and four destroyers struck at the unescorted merchantmen proceeding along India's east coast. In a swift raid that lasted only from the afternoon of 5 April until the early morning of the 7th, this force sank eighteen vessels totalling over 93,000 tons and *Ryujo*'s Kates attacked the Indian ports of Coconada and Vizagapatam, doing little damage but causing the flight of the civilian population almost to the last man. So great was the panic caused that all sailings from India's east coast ports were suspended forthwith and not resumed until the end of the month and a false air-raid warning at Madras was sufficient to cause a major evacuation.

It was an astonishing achievement in a very short time by a fairly small force and showed clearly the demoralization prevalent in Britain's eastern possessions. Nor was this improved by the appearance in the Indian Ocean of a much larger squadron commanded by Vice Admiral Nagumo. Of the six carriers that had assaulted Pearl Harbor, *Kaga* had returned to Japan with engine trouble, but *Akagi*, *Soryu*, *Hiryu*, *Shokaku* and *Zuikaku* were all present, escorted by four battleships, two heavy cruisers, one light cruiser and eleven destroyers. On 5 April, Commander Fuchida led his airmen against the great port of Colombo, and on the 9th he turned his attention to the Royal Navy base at Trincomalee.

After their spectacular achievements at Pearl Harbor and Port Darwin, the Japanese were disappointed by the much lesser results of both these raids, but they gained ample compensation at the expense of Britain's Eastern Fleet. This time it was Japan's Val dive-bombers that proved horribly effective and during operations in the vicinity of Ceylon they sank light carrier *Hermes*, heavy cruisers *Dorsetshire* and *Cornwall*, Australian destroyer *Vampire* and several smaller vessels. Not one of Nagumo's ships was even slightly damaged.

Yet had Nagumo been able to foresee the future, he would have realized that his sortie, for all its tactical successes, had brought no strategic benefit. On the contrary, he had wasted precious time that his carriers could have better used in countering the American build-up in the Pacific, to which they now belatedly returned. Had his raid been followed by an invasion of Ceylon, as many of Japan's Naval General Staff strongly favoured, then it would have been abundantly justified, but any chance that the Imperial Army would agree to this was ended by the comparative lack of damage inflicted at Colombo and Trincomalee and the spirited resistance, acknowledged by Fuchida's airmen, put up by the hopelessly outnumbered RAF Hurricanes and Fleet Air Arm Fulmars. The threat to Ceylon would never be renewed.

Unfortunately, the British could not foresee the future either and the losses of the Eastern Fleet and the apparent danger to Ceylon greatly alarmed Churchill. The prime minister could see all too clearly the consequences of an occupation of Ceylon. From that island, the Japanese could have threatened several vital convoy routes: that in the Bay of Bengal, interference with which would have necessitated supplying Allied forces on the India/Burma front overland; that carrying oil from the Middle East; and that bringing reinforcements to Eighth Army, the severance of which would probably have led to the collapse of the Allied cause in the Mediterranean and provided the final evidence of Churchill's folly in neglecting the Far East for the sake of gaining a victory in North Africa.

These eventualities would, happily, never occur but it would be a long time before Churchill could know this for certain, and in the meantime bad news continued to come in from Burma where Japanese dominance at sea ensured the safe arrival of their reinforcements at Rangoon. By 19 April Lieutenant General Sakurai's 33rd Division had received its third regiment, the 213th, and Lieutenant General Mutaguchi's 18th Division from Singapore, the 56th Infantry Division, two tank regiments, two heavy field artillery regiments and several supporting units had all arrived to more than double the strength of Lieutenant General Iida's Fifteenth Army.

Reinforcements of aircraft had also all but doubled the strength of Japan's Army Air Force in Burma, and by the end of March a series of raids on RAF bases had virtually eliminated the Allied warplanes in the colony and caused the few that remained to withdraw to India. Though the now unopposed Japanese airmen made surprisingly few attacks on British and Commonwealth soldiers, they devastated the Burmese cities and thus increased the flood of terrified fugitives. Their reconnaissance machines also kept Iida well informed of his enemies' actions, while his own movements remained undetected.

There was no prospect of the Allied losses of aircraft being made good, but during March the soldiers of the Burma Army were joined by Chinese troops. The Fifth Chinese Army moved into the valley of the Sittang, the Sixth Chinese Army entered the Shan States in the east of Burma and the Sixty-Sixth Chinese Army took up station on Burma's northern frontier to act as a reserve. Unhappily, their arrival was very much a mixed blessing.

For a start, a Chinese 'army' was at best equivalent to a British corps in manpower and vastly weaker in equipment, transport and supporting units. A Chinese division was scarcely more powerful than a normal British brigade. As for the calibre of the troops, this was perhaps best summed up by Chiang Kai-shek who considered that they should never engage the Japanese unless they outnumbered them by at least five to one. Chiang was also understandably indignant that his men would receive no support or protection from the air, and hinted that China might 'be forced to reconsider her position'.

The presence of Chinese troops in the Sittang valley did bring one immediate tactical benefit for the British and Commonwealth troops. Iida directed his 55th, 56th and 18th divisions against them, leaving only Sakurai's 33rd Division to oppose the Burma Army in the valley of the Irrawaddy. Yet paradoxically, this caused immense harm to the British. Lieutenant General Alexander was a fine far-sighted strategist. He rightly realized that with their command of the air and their ability to provide reinforcements at will, the Japanese could not now be prevented from seizing Burma. Had he been opposed by the full Japanese strength, it seems that he would have conducted an orderly retreat, but one as rapid as was consistent with the need to destroy such strategic prizes as the Yenangyaung oilfields before the enemy reached there.

As it was, the arrival of the Chinese, while not deceiving Alexander into believing that Burma could be held, did make him feel that he might 'impose the maximum delay on the enemy and make him expend resources which he might have employed elsewhere.' In any case, political considerations meant that no British retreat, however sensible or desirable, could be tolerated if it would risk leaving Chinese troops 'out on a limb'. In effect, Alexander's every action had to be co-ordinated with those of the Chinese and this not only restricted his freedom of movement, but also meant that his left flank was in constant danger of being exposed by the defeat of his unreliable allies.

To make matters worse, on 19 March all British and Commonwealth units were combined as Burma Corps. Its leader, who would in future exercise tactical control, was Lieutenant General William Slim, an extremely determined and aggressive officer but unfortunately one with very different intentions from Alexander, mainly because at this time he, like Wavell, badly underestimated the Japanese, although, unlike Wavell, he would never admit this. Major General Lunt reveals that Brigadier Bourke who commanded 2nd Burma Brigade, in which Lunt was then serving, returned from a conference with Slim shortly after the latter's appointment, and informed his officers that 'it was the Corps Commander's intention to recapture Rangoon before the monsoon broke in mid-May.'

Slim's memoirs, *Defeat into Victory*, discreetly omit any reference to this intention but they do confirm that he wished to halt the British retreat, considering it to be 'dangerous'. They also record repeated examples of his desire of 'counter-attacking at the earliest possible opportunity' or of 'staging a counter-offensive' or striking 'a counter-blow'. Slim does admit that his plans could be 'a little ambitious'.

In reality, Slim's counter-attacks were the height of folly. They had to be carried out unsupported from the air and by formations that had been weakened and demoralized by previous misfortunes. Moreover, even if they had gained a temporary success, this would have been rendered futile by the Japanese threat to their left flank. If Burma Corps could not halt, let alone drive back Sakurai's single 33rd Division – as in fact proved to be the case – then the Chinese could hardly be expected to withstand the assaults of three Japanese divisions. If the Chinese gave way, then the further south Slim's counter-attacks progressed, the more likely it would be that the troops making them would be cut off, and the greater the number of those troops, the more who would be endangered.

It is not surprising, therefore, that Burma Corps suffered a further series of humiliations. Yet, astonishingly, as late as 19 April, when 1st Burma Division had just experienced a particularly horrific defeat at Yenangyaung and the Chinese were on the verge of total disintegration and interested only in regaining their own country, Slim still believed that 'we might turn the tables on the Japanese and thus avoid abandoning Burma.' Fortunately, Alexander thought otherwise. He was normally reluctant to interfere with the dispositions of his subordinates – for which Slim showed no gratitude either at the time or later – but he now intervened decisively. On 25 April he notified Slim that Burma was to be abandoned forthwith.

By this action, says Major General Lunt, Alexander 'certainly saved the Burma Army'. Two days earlier, he had advised Wavell that the state of his supplies made it impossible to retire into China as Churchill had suggested for political reasons; instead he would make for Imphal in India. In the process the Burma Army suffered further misfortunes, but on 12 May the monsoon broke in full fury, finally ending the Japanese advance. The last stragglers reached Imphal on the 20th. Five months and thirteen days had elapsed since the attack on Pearl Harbor.

At a press conference, both Wavell and Alexander referred to 'a glorious retreat'. Neither can really have believed this and Alexander would later honestly describe it as 'a complete military defeat'. Though the Burma Army had survived to provide the basis on which the British could build up their strength for future operations, its losses had been immense. A total of 4,033 British, Indian, Burmese or Gurkha soldiers had been killed or wounded in combat – about a third of them killed – and disease had caused still greater casualties. Burma Army's equipment had been reduced to 50 lorries, 30 jeeps, 28 guns and a solitary tank. The Chinese losses have not been recorded, but were certainly much higher.

Much more shameful was the fact that the Burma Army had lost 9,430 men who had either surrendered or deserted. The Japanese, though they had had far fewer soldiers killed and wounded than the British and Chinese combined, had in fact had more casualties than the British alone: 4,597 to be exact. Not one man, however, had surrendered or deserted. As in Malaya and at Singapore, the British had been 'outmatched by better soldiers'.

British prestige would never recover from this series of disasters in the Far East. The majority of Britain's Asian subjects had supported her rule because they trusted that she would protect them. To their amazement and horror, they now saw their cities reduced to ruin and thousands of their peoples slaughtered by war, disease and starvation. It was an experience that could never be forgotten.

Nor could the memory of that experience be removed by the British reconquest of most of Burma in the last year of the war. At the time that this took place, much of Japan's military strength and almost all her aerial strength had been removed from Burma to fight in more vital areas. As General Sir David Fraser points out, the Japanese 'were on almost every occasion outnumbered – sometimes by a large margin.' Crushing them by overwhelming force cost money, material and, most important, men's lives, but did little to affect the outcome of the war and nothing to restore the reputation the British had lost in 1942.

For the British servicemen who were responsible for the recapture of Burma, it is doubtful if this mattered much. They had been driven mainly by that most natural but most unworthy of motives: a desire to gain their revenge on the enemies who had shamed them and inflicted disgusting treatment on their captured comrades. Having achieved this, they wanted only to go home. Slim relates that when he asked any soldier what he was, the man would report not his occupation or his regiment but 'the number of years and months he had served in the East, and the unspoken question in his eyes was: "How many more?"'

In January 1946, the ground crews on a number of RAF stations in the vicinity of Calcutta were so exasperated by the delays in their repatriation that they mutinied. 'Went on strike' would perhaps be a fairer description of their attitude, for although they refused to obey orders, their officers were never threatened but continued to receive formal respect, and they resumed their duties after being reassured that their demands would be met. Nonetheless, it had been made clear that if the lands of the Far East no longer wanted British rule, the British were no longer interested in keeping it.

It seems unlikely that Brooke was greatly surprised by these developments, for shortly after the fall of Singapore he had noted in his diary: 'If the Army cannot fight better than it is doing at present we shall deserve to lose our Empire.' Churchill, however, does not appear to have anticipated them. Later in 1942 he would announce firmly: 'I have not become the King's First Minister in order to preside over the liquidation of the British Empire. For that task, if ever it were prescribed, someone else would have to be found.'

Churchill, though he did not realize it, had in fact already presided over the catastrophes that would result in the liquidation of the British Empire. He would at least be spared the task of formally arranging this since his all-party National Government came to an end on the conclusion of the war in Europe, and in the resulting General Election he was heavily defeated and accordingly ceased to be prime minister. Thereafter he could only look on in anguish as Britain's Far Eastern possessions not only obtained self-government – that he had recognized as inevitable – but became republics with the king no longer head of state; as the magnificent Indian army was broken up when the subcontinent was partitioned; and as Burma left the Commonwealth altogether. Such were the final fruits of Britain's worst ever month: February 1942.

Bibliography

Allen, Louis, *Burma: The Longest War 1941–45* (J.M. Dent, 1984)

Allen, Louis, *Singapore 1941–42* (Davis-Poynter Limited, 1977)

Arnold-Forster, Mark, *The World at War* (Collins, 1973)

Auchinleck, Field Marshal Sir Claude, 'Operations in Middle East 1/11/41 to 15/8/42', *London Gazette Supplement* 1948

Behrendt, Hans-Otto, *Rommel's Intelligence in the Desert Campaign* (Kimbers, 1985)

Bickers, Richard Townshend, *The Desert Air War 1939–45* (Leo Cooper, 1991)

Bowyer, Chaz, *Eugene Esmonde VC DSO* (Kimbers, 1983)

Bryant, Sir Arthur, *The Turn of the Tide 1939–1943* (Collins, 1959)

Callahan, Raymond, *Burma 1942–45* (Davis-Poynter Limited, 1978)

Cameron, Ian, *Red Duster, White Ensign* (Frederick Muller, 1959)

Carell, Paul, *The Foxes of the Desert: The Story of the Afrika Korps* (Macdonalds, 1960)

Carew, Tim, *The Longest Retreat: The Burma Campaign 1942* (Hamish Hamilton, 1969)

Carver, Field Marshal Lord, *Dilemmas of the Desert War: A New Look at the Libyan Campaign 1940–1942* (Batsford, 1986)

Carver, Field Marshal Lord, *Tobruk* (Batsford, 1964)

Churchill, Winston S., *The Second World War. Volume III: The Grand Alliance* (Cassell, 1950). *Volume IV: The Hinge of Fate* (Cassell, 1951)

Connaughton, Richard, *Shrouded Secrets: Japan's War on Mainland Australia 1942–44* (Brasseys, 1994)

Connell, John, *Auchinleck* (Cassell, 1959)

Costello, John, *The Pacific War* (Collins, 1981)

D'Albas, Captain Andrieu, *Death of a Navy* (Robert Hale, 1957)

De Guingand, Major General Sir Francis, *Operation Victory* (Hodder & Stoughton, 1947)

Dull, Paul S., *A Battle History of the Imperial Japanese Navy (1941–1945)* (Patrick Stephens, 1978)

Falk, Stanley L., *Seventy Days to Singapore: The Malayan Campaign 1941–1942* (Robert Hale, 1975)

Fraser, General Sir David, *And We Shall Shock Them: The British Army in the Second World War* (Hodder & Stoughton, 1983)

Fuller, Major General J.F.C., *The Decisive Battles of the Western World* (Volume 3) (Eyre & Spottiswoode, 1957)

Fuller, Major General J.F.C., *The Second World War 1939–1945* (Eyre & Spottiswoode, 1948. Revised Edition, 1954)

Holmes, Richard & Kemp, Anthony, *The Bitter End: The Fall of Singapore 1941–42* (Anthony Bird Publications, 1982)

Jackson, General Sir William, *The North African Campaign 1940–43* (Batsford, 1975)

Kahn, David, *The Codebreakers* (Weidenfeld & Nicolson, 1973)

Kelly, Terence, *Battle for Palembang* (Robert Hale, 1985)

Kelly, Terence, *Hurricane over the Jungle* (Kimbers, 1977)

Kemp, Lieutenant Commander P.K., *Victory at Sea* (Frederick Muller, 1957)

Leasor, James, *Singapore: The Battle that Changed the World* (Hodder & Stoughton, 1968)

Lewin, Ronald, *The Life and Death of the Afrika Korps* (Batsford, 1977)

Lewin, Ronald, *Rommel as Military Commander* (Batsford, 1968)

Lewin, Ronald, *Ultra Goes to War: The Secret Story* (Hutchinson, 1978)

Liddell Hart, Captain B.H., *History of the Second World War* (Cassell, 1970)

Liddell Hart, Captain B.H., *The Tanks: The History of the Royal Tank Regiment and its Predecessors* (Cassell, 1959)

Lunt, Major General James, *A Hell of a Licking: The Retreat from Burma 1941–2* (Collins, 1986)

Macintyre, Captain Donald, *The Battle of the Atlantic* (Batsford, 1961)

Macintyre, Captain Donald, *The Battle for the Mediterranean* (Batsford, 1964)

Macintyre, Captain Donald, *The Battle for the Pacific* (Batsford, 1966)
Mellenthin, Major General F.W. von, *Panzer Battles* (Cassell, 1955)
Menzies, Sir Robert, *Afternoon Light* (Cassell, 1967)
Moorehead, Alan, *The Desert War: The North African Campaign 1940–1943* (Hamish Hamilton, 1965)
Morison, Samuel Eliot, *The Two-Ocean War: A Short History of the United States Navy in the Second World War* (Little, Brown & Co., 1963)
Nicolson, Nigel, *Alex: The Life of Field Marshal Earl Alexander of Tunis* (Weidenfeld & Nicolson, 1973)
Owen, Lieutenant Colonel Frank, *The Fall of Singapore* (Michael Joseph, 1960)
Owen, Roderic, *The Desert Air Force* (Hutchinson, 1948)
Playfair, Major General I.S.O. with Flynn, Captain F.C., Molony, Brigadier C.J.C. and Gleave, Group Captain T.P., *The Mediterranean and Middle East. Volume III: British Fortunes Reach their Lowest Ebb* (HMSO, 1960)
Potter, E.B. & Nimitz, Fleet Admiral Chester W., *The Great Sea War* (George W. Harrap & Co., 1961)
Richards, Denis, *Royal Air Force 1939–1945. Volume I: The Fight at Odds* (HMSO, 1953)
Richards, Denis & Saunders, Hilary St G., *Royal Air Force 1939–1945. Volume II: The Fight Avails* (HMSO, 1954)
Robertson, John, *Australia at War 1939–1945* (Collins, 1960)
Robertson, Terence, *Channel Dash* (Evans Brothers, 1958)
Rommel, Field Marshal Erwin (ed. Liddell Hart, Captain B.H.), *The Rommel Papers* (Collins, 1953)
Roskill, Captain S.W., *The Navy at War 1939–1945* (Collins, 1960)
Roskill, Captain S.W., *The War at Sea. Volume II: The Period of Balance* (HMSO, 1956)
Shores, Christopher & Cull, Brian with Izawa, Yasuho, *Bloody Shambles. Volume I: The Drift to War to the Fall of Singapore* (Grub Street, 1992). *Volume II: The Defence of Sumatra to the Fall of Burma* (Grub Street, 1993)
Shores, Christopher & Cull, Brian with Maliza, Nicola, *Malta: The Spitfire Year 1942* (Grub Street, 1991)

Shores, Christopher & Ring, Hans, *Fighters over the Desert: The Air Battles in the Western Desert June 1940 to December 1942* (Neville Spearman, 1969)

Simson, Brigadier Ivan, *Singapore: Too Little, Too Late* (Leo Cooper, 1970)

Slim, Field Marshal Sir William, *Defeat into Victory* (Cassell, 1956)

Smith, Brigadier E.D., *Battle for Burma* (Batsford, 1979)

Stewart, Adrian, *The Campaigns of Alexander of Tunis 1940–1945* (Pen & Sword, 2008)

Stewart, Adrian, *The Early Battles of Eighth Army* (Leo Cooper, 2002)

Stewart, Adrian, *The Underrated Enemy: Britain's War with Japan December 1941 – May 1942* (Kimbers, 1987)

Strawson, Major General Sir John, *The Battle for North Africa* (Batsford, 1969)

Thomas, David A., *Battle of the Java Sea* (Andre Deutsch, 1968)

Thomas, David A., *Japan's War at Sea: Pearl Harbor to the Coral Sea* (Andre Deutsch, 1978)

Tomlinson, Michael, *The Most Dangerous Moment* (Kimbers, 1976)

Tsuji, Colonel Masanobu, *Singapore: The Japanese Version* (Mayflower-Dell, 1966)

Willmott, H.P., *Empires in the Balance: Japanese and Allied Pacific Strategies to April 1942* (Naval Institute Press, Annapolis, 1982)

Woodman, Richard, *Malta Convoys 1940–1943* (John Murray, 2000)

Wykeham, Air Marshal Sir Peter, *Fighter Command* (Putnams, 1960)

Index